The Impact of Trade and Domestic Policy Reforms in India: A CGE Modeling Approach

SIE *Studies in International Economics* includes works dealing with the theory; empirical analysis; political, economic, and legal aspects; and evaluation of international policies and institutions.

Keith E. Maskus, Peter M. Hooper, Edward E. Leamer, and J. David Richardson, Editors
Quiet Pioneering: Robert M. Stern and His International Economic Legacy

Bjarne S. Jensen and Kar-yiu Wong, Editors
Dynamics, Economic Growth, and International Trade

Kala Marathe Krishna and Ling Hui Tan
Rags and Riches: Implementing Apparel Quotas under the Multi-Fibre Arrangement

Alan V. Deardorff and Robert M. Stern
Measurement of Nontariff Barriers

Thomas Cottier and Petros C. Mavroidis, Editors
The World Trade Forum, Volume I: State Trading in the Twenty-First Century

Rajesh Chadha, Sanjib Pohit, Alan V. Deardorff, and Robert M. Stern
The Impact of Trade and Domestic Policy Reforms in India: A CGE Modeling Approach

Alan V. Deardorff and Robert M. Stern, Editors
Constituent Interests and U.S. Trade Policies

Gary R. Saxonhouse and T. N. Srinivasan, Editors
Development, Duality, and the International Economic Regime: Essays in Honor of Gustav Ranis

The Impact of Trade and Domestic Policy Reforms in India: A CGE Modeling Approach

Rajesh Chadha, Sanjib Pohit,
Alan V. Deardorff, and Robert M. Stern

Ann Arbor

THE UNIVERSITY OF MICHIGAN PRESS

Published in the United States of America by
The University of Michigan Press
Manufactured in the United States of America
♾ Printed on acid-free paper

2001 2000 1999 1998 4 3 2 1

A CIP catalog record for this book is available from the British Library.

Library of Congress Cataloging-in-Publication data applied for
ISBN 0-472-10933-2

Contents

Foreword

The process of major economic reforms undertaken in the Indian economy has completed more than six years of implementation. The economy has entered into a new phase of development directed towards becoming globally competitive through the opening of trade, foreign investment, and technology inflows. The unilateral reform measures in the industrial and trade policies of India along with reforms in the tax regime represent a significant departure from the policy framework of the past four decades and are important to the future course of the Indian economy.

The basic objective of this study is to evaluate the comparative static effects of selected trade and domestic policy reforms on trade, output, domestic prices, economic welfare and the intersectoral allocation of resources. The major reforms analyzed relate to reductions in tariff and nontariff barriers to trade along with rationalization of the tax regime. A computable general equilibrium (CGE) model of the Indian economy has been constructed for the purpose of analysis.

The results indicate that import liberalization enhances the welfare of the economy, but the effect gets further enlarged if exports are also liberalized simultaneously. This is particularly true of the agricultural sectors. The freeing of prices in the sectors that were under some form of administered price controls in the base year (1989–90) significantly enlarges the welfare effect. The economy becomes more efficient through better allocation of land, labor and capital across different producing sectors with increases in the returns to each of these factors of production. Output as well as exports are expected to register the largest increases in five sectors, viz. clothing, leather products, footwear, non-metallic mineral products and glass products. These sectors are the major gainers from improving scale economies. The major sectors in terms of declines in output as well as resource-usage are expected to be non-ferrous metals, non-electrical machinery, and mining and quarrying. However, the mining and quarrying sector may not decline if prices in the administered sectors are not freed. In the case of the agricultural sector, resources are expected to move from cereals to other crops. The rationalization of the existing structure of indirect taxes (mainly excise) and subsidies is expected to further benefit the factors of production and enhance overall welfare.

The active collaboration between NCAER, New Delhi, and the University of Michigan, Ann Arbor, has been immensely helpful in making the timely completion of this study possible. We would like to put on record our sincere thanks to Robert M. Stern and Alan V. Deardorff of the University of Michigan and Drusilla K. Brown of Tufts University for their academic support.

We acknowledge with gratitude the critical comments and suggestions provided to us by the members of the Advisory Committee for this Project. Thomas W. Hertel of Purdue University, K. L. Krishna and V. Pandit of the Delhi School of Economics and Shashanka Bhide of NCAER have played a very special role in this regard.

The analysis of the India CGE model developed in this study has been made possible through the use of the General Equilibrium Modelling Package (GEMPACK) Software developed at Monash University, Melbourne, Australia, by Jill Harrison and Ken Pearson. We are extremely thankful to Ken Pearson for his prompt and active support in making this software package operative on NCAER's UNIX computer.

We would like to thank N. Sangeeta, K. A. Siddiqui, Sujata Mishra, Sarika Pruthi and J. M. Chawla of the NCAER and Alan K. Fox and Judith Jackson of the University of Michigan for their able research and software support and Judith Jackson for typing and editorial assistance.

S. L. Rao, former Director General of the NCAER, was instrumental in getting this study started and took keen interest in its progress.

Financial support for the study was provided by the USAID, New Delhi. Mr. Jon O'Rourke and Dr. Madhumita Gupta, both from USAID, deserve our special thanks.

Rakesh Mohan
Dircctor Gcncral, NCAER

February 1998

CHAPTER 1

Introduction

1.1 About the Present Study

The process of major economic reforms undertaken in the Indian economy has now completed six years of implementation. The economy has entered into a new phase of development directed towards becoming globally competitive through opening up to trade, foreign investment, and technology inflows. The unilateral reforms of the trade and domestic policies of India, along with reforms of the tax regime since 1991, represent a significant departure from the policy framework of the previous four decades and are important to the future course of the Indian economy. There is an ongoing debate in India regarding the likely impacts of sectoral reforms on output, employment and other variables that affect the economic well-being of the country's population. It thus becomes important to evaluate the effects of such policy reforms on factor prices, output, and trade, along with inter-sectoral movement of resources, viz. land, labor, and capital. To address these issues, we use a 34-sector computable general equilibrium (CGE) model for India. We hope that our analysis will provide a more solid underpinning for the ongoing policy debate.

1.2 Policy Relevance

India entered into an era of ambitious industrialization during the mid-1950s with the Mahalanobis strategy of development as its basis. The emphasis was on import substitution, heavy industries and a central role for the public sector. Export pessimism was widely prevalent. The trade policy regime was highly protectionist and regulated through quantitative controls on imports. Tariff rates were exceptionally high. Domestic industry, heavily insulated from international competition, was under strict regulation.

A beginning was made towards liberalization of India's trade policy regime during the late 1970s, and this liberalization gained some momentum during the latter half of the 1980s. The Committees led by P.C. Alexander (1977), Abid Hussain (1984), and Narasimham (1985) influenced Indian thinking on trade policy reform by emphasizing two major points: (1) there was a need to develop an efficient system that would make exports less costly and more profitable; and (2) there was a need to move away from a discretionary system of quantitative import controls to a system based on tariffs. The Long Term Fiscal Policy, announced in 1985, envisaged the eventual removal of import licensing from all imports except consumer goods and also proposed simplification of the complex tariff structure. Quantitative restrictions were in fact being gradually removed along with expansion in the open general license (OGL) list of imports. The imports of various capital goods and raw materials became freer as these were put on the OGL list along with reduction in their tariff rates. However, the changes that took place up to July 1991 were quite small by comparison to what was needed. The dominant view continued to be that if a good could be produced in India, then it should be protected from import competition irrespective of its cost of production. Thus, despite all these measures, the Indian economy remained a highly protected economy at the end of the 1980s (see World Bank, 1989).

India commenced its major thrust towards globalization in July 1991, triggered by the pressure of crisis in its external sector and a concurrent fiscal deficit. A program of macroeconomic stabilization was initiated that included reducing the fiscal deficit, controlling the money supply, and correcting the overvalued currency by a major devaluation of the rupee. The rupee was subsequently made partially convertible in 1992–93, fully convertible on trade account in 1993–94, and fully convertible on current account in 1994–95. Many overdue microeconomic/sectoral reforms with a medium-term perspective were also launched. Major structural reforms were introduced in the industrial and trade policy regimes and in the financial sector with a view to improving the efficiency, productivity and international competitiveness of India's manufacturing sector.[1]

It has now become widely accepted that, in order to achieve the desired results, India has to transform itself into an internationally competitive economy open to trade and foreign investment. Significant changes in the industrial policy regime have already led to industrial delicensing and a larger role for the private sector. Changes in trade policy have involved abolishing import licensing (except for imports of consumer goods) as well as reductions in import duties. Reforms have also been initiated towards streamlining the structure of indirect taxes in India. With these trade and industrial policy reforms, India has entered a new era with a more competitive industrial environment in which entrepreneurs are expected to respond more to the signals of the market than to bureaucratic controls and the need to skirt around them.

The economy appears to have responded well to the ongoing process of economic reforms. GDP has grown by more than 6.5% per annum between 1992 and 1997. The Central Government's fiscal deficit as a proportion of GDP has declined significantly. The rate of gross domestic savings has risen substantially. The average rate of inflation has been below double digits. Both exports and imports have grown significantly faster during this period.[2]

The issues that we will analyze below have immense policy relevance for India. For example, Indian policy makers need to know the likely direction of intersectoral changes that would result when India undertakes unilateral trade and industrial policy reforms, and when its industrial structure becomes more internationally competitive. The analysis may also help to identify the relative strengths of sectors in making decisions with regard to future investments and the implications for expanding and contracting sectors in terms of employment.

1.3 Objective of the Study

The basic objective of this study is to evaluate the comparative static effects of selected trade and domestic policy reforms on output, trade, factor prices, economic welfare and the intersectoral allocation of resources. A computable general equilibrium (CGE) model of the Indian economy has been developed for this purpose.

We focus in particular on changes in tariffs and non-tariff barriers (NTBs) under three alternative assumptions: (1) the economy retains certain product market imperfections (state monopolies and administered prices) as these existed in 1989–90; (2) the economy is free from such distortions; and (3) the economy is free from such distortions and an attempt is also made to rationalize the indirect-tax regime. Our computational analysis includes the following aspects of the reforms:

i) Import Reforms: these refer to reductions in tariffs and NTBs on imports;
ii) Import and Export Reforms: these refer to the above mentioned import reforms plus reduction in NTBs on exports.

The first set of simulations refers to trade liberalization while retaining the product market imperfections. The state monopolies and the administered-price sectors continue to operate in the same way. The domestic policy reforms are thus assumed to maintain the status quo. We refer to this as the "administered version" of the model. The results of such analysis are thus based on the assumption that domestic policy with respect to the product market imperfections remains unchanged.

The second set of simulations refers to trade liberalization under the assumption that the domestic reforms have already taken place. We refer to this as the "market version" of the model. It is assumed that before we introduce trade reforms, as indicated above, the economy has already removed the product market imperfections. Thus all the sectors that were under state monopoly in 1989–90 are assumed to have been opened up to private competition, such that petroleum products and iron and steel operate under monopolistic competition, while mining and quarrying, electricity, gas and water, and rail transport operate under perfect competition. Accordingly, prices are no longer taken to be "administered" in these sectors. We also assume that the sectors that were under some kind of administered price regime in 1989–90 now determine their own prices. This amounts to doing away with administered prices in two agricultural sectors, viz.

paddy and wheat, and in three manufacturing sectors, viz. paper products, fertilizer, and non-ferrous metals. The paddy and wheat sectors are assumed to be perfectly competitive while the three manufacturing sectors are assumed to be monopolistically competitive. Further, domestic capital is assumed mobile across all sectors.

The third set of simulations refers to trade liberalization under the "market version" of the model along with reducing subsidies (by increasing other net indirect taxes) in the agricultural sectors, fertilizer, and electricity, gas and water supply, and also reducing excise duties (by reducing net indirect taxes) on the remaining sectors of the Indian economy. Thus, these changes in indirect taxes are superimposed on the experiments with import and export liberalization under the domestically liberalized economy (market version) as discussed above in the second set of simulations.

1.4 Major Results

The results indicate that the import liberalization enhances the welfare of the Indian economy, and that the effect is further enlarged if exports are also liberalized simultaneously. This is particularly true of the agricultural sectors. The freeing of prices in the sectors that were under some form of administered price controls in the base year (1989–90) adds noticeably to the welfare gain. The economy becomes more efficient through reallocation of land, labor and capital across different producing sectors with increases in the real returns to each of the factors of production. The rationalization of the existing structure of indirect taxes (mainly excise) and subsidies is expected to benefit further the factors of production and enhance overall welfare. Although such ex-ante analysis may not be replicated ex-post due to various macroeconomic and other factors that our model does not capture, the positive results nevertheless go a long way in establishing the credibility of the reforms process.

1.5 Plan of the Study

Following this introduction, chapter 2 provides an overview of India's development experience during the period 1951–1991 and its transition towards a more open economy since 1991. It includes a discussion of the major restrictive features of the Indian economy towards the end of the 1980s, viz. the regulations on production and trade along with the working of the Indian factor markets. It also provides an overview of the reforms undertaken since 1991. Chapter 3 provides detailed documentation of the multi-sectoral India CGE model along with its assumptions, equations and discussion of the closure issue. A comparison of the India CGE model with other models of the Indian economy is also highlighted in this chapter. Chapter 4 provides a detailed account of the model implementation. It presents the data and the parameters required to run the model along with the solution procedure. Chapter 5 deals with policy simulations based on an assessment of the present and the future direction of India's economic reforms, particularly with reference to target levels of tariffs, quotas, production taxes and subsidies, and domestic policy reforms. We also perform sensitivity analysis of the model. We conclude in chapter 6 with a discussion of the implications of our study for further research to expand our CGE modeling structure.

CHAPTER 2

India's Economic Transition

As already mentioned, our objective in this study is to evaluate the impact of India's economic reforms, undertaken since 1991, on various aspects of the Indian economy. Before proceeding with our analysis, it is useful first to discuss the relevant features of the Indian economy towards the end of the 1980s. A slow process of trade and industrial reforms was carried out during the 1980s in the form of some decontrol within a highly regulated policy regime. However, the major thrust toward globalizing the Indian economy has been provided by the reforms process that commenced in July 1991. After examining the salient features of the Indian economy from the 1950s to the end of the 1980s, we then consider the post-1991 reform measures particularly in trade and industrial policies along with the intended restructuring of indirect taxes.

2.1 India's Development Experience (1951–1991)

2.1.1 Introduction

India was an under-developed economy when it attained its independence from British rule on August 15, 1947. The aftereffects of the Second World War and partition with Pakistan had shattered its economy markedly. Nearly 85 percent of India's population lived in villages, with 70 percent of its working population being engaged in agriculture and related pursuits using traditional and low productivity techniques. The primary sector contributed about 56 percent of GDP in 1950–51 compared with a 15 percent share of the secondary sector and the remaining 28 percent being contributed by the tertiary sector.

India's development strategy, following the adoption of a new Indian Constitution on January 26, 1950, was based on the concept of a self-reliant welfare state with the declared social objective of economic growth with equitable distribution to be achieved in a democratic political framework. Such a framework ruled out any radical changes in the production and distribution process of the existing capitalist institutions. Thus, the three broad objectives of the Indian development strategy were: economic growth; self reliance; and social justice.

In order to achieve its declared objectives, India opted to introduce far reaching measures of economic planning. This task was entrusted to the Indian

Planning Commission which was established in 1950. The Commission had only advisory and recommendatory powers with implementation being left to the executive organs of the government consisting of various ministries at the Centre along with the state governments.

India's economic planning was influenced by the economic thinking of the then Prime Minister Pandit Jawahar Lal Nehru and the economist Prof. P. C. Mahalanobis who were impressed by the Soviet planning experience. However, India did not adopt totalitarian political control of the society and complete state ownership of the means of production, the two major features of the Soviet planning. India retained instead the institution of private ownership of property and the means of production, along with the freedom to utilize them in economic activity within the legal and constitutional framework and with private profit as a motive force. The state was expected to play an active positive role by providing social and economic infrastructure. The Mahalanobis strategy emphasized the development of basic and heavy industry to encourage import substitution.

India adopted the choice of a "mixed economy" in an attempt to meet the aforementioned objectives of self-reliant growth with social justice. The mixed economy in India's context can be characterized as essentially a capitalist economy modified by the direct participation as well as intervention by the state in economic activity (see Tendulkar, 1981). The state was expected to play a proactive role in economic activity by promoting economic growth as well as distributional objectives without resorting to coercive means. The state was to influence the pace as well as the composition of economic activity through expansion of the public sector. The democratic framework permitted private ownership of property and the means of production. The private owners were free to utilize their assets to earn profit but only under the constraints imposed by the regulatory economic policy and the legal and constitutional framework. Though the state was not identified with any particular interest groups, many such groups were active in seeking to influence state actions in their favor.

The operation of the state was promised on three classes of economic instruments: aggregate fiscal and monetary policies; market intervention without undertaking direct production; and extending public ownership of the means of production. The government was expected to use these instruments to control the growth and composition of the private sector in the interest of equity. It was believed that the private sector was either unwilling or unable to invest at a scale required in heavy industries and infrastructure in the face of the nascent capital markets and long gestation periods in some of these areas, and that private entrepreneurs would also demand a higher risk premium than was considered to be socially justified. The extension of the public ownership of means of production was expected to provide the most effective method for enabling the democratic state to encourage growth with equitable distribution, thus reducing the concentration of economic power. The public was expected to act as a model employer so as to provide direction to the policies of the private sector and at the same time to generate investible surpluses to promote the growth of capital in the economy.

The public sector control over production and distribution of certain widely used intermediate inputs like coal, steel, and electricity was expected to enable it to influence the composition of private economic activity in a socially desirable direction. The role of the public sector was emphasized in the context of the Mahalanobis growth strategy as contained in the Second Five Year Plan (1956–61). In view of the then prevailing export pessimism, it was believed that long-term growth could be achieved through import substitution with domestic capacity creation biased in favor of producing capital goods.

The growth experience of the Indian economy during the period 1951–1991 may be divided into three phases for agriculture and industry. **Phase I** (1951–1965) was the phase of commencement of the five-year plans. It was a period of rapid industrial growth. Agricultural output grew during this period due to increase in the net cropped area rather than increases in yield. Institutional reforms were the major pre-occupation of the policy makers in this phase. **Phase II** (1965–1980) turned out to be a period of industrial deceleration due to slowdown in public investment and resulting inadequate infrastructure investment, poor management of the infrastructure, slow growth of agricultural incomes and resulting slow growth in demand for industrial products, and restrictive industrial and foreign trade policies leading to a high-cost industrial structure (see Ahluwalia, 1985). In the agricultural sector, this phase witnessed the beginning of a new agricultural strategy based on the use of superior technology. Though agricultural output increased due to increasing yields, the benefits remained confined to certain specific crops, regions, and classes of farmers. **Phase III** (1980–1991) witnessed a rapid growth of industry. The crops, regions, and the classes of farmers who had been lagging during the first decade of Green Revolution started catching up during the 1980s.

The experience of the period 1951–1991 has been summarized by Bhagwati (1997) with the following "sobering conclusions."

India had started out in the 1950s with:

- high growth rates;
- openness to trade and investment;
- a promotional state;
- social expenditure;
- social expenditure awareness;
- confidence that the poverty would be seriously dented by growth;
- macro stability;
- optimism; and hence
- admiration of the world.

But by the end of the 1980s India was characterized by:

- low growth rates;[3]
- closure to trade and investment;
- a license-obsessed, restrictive state;
- inability to sustain social expenditures;
- loss of confidence in the efficacy of growth in reducing poverty;

- macro instability, indeed crisis;
- pessimism; and therefore
- marginalization of India in world affairs.

2.1.2 Industry

The foundation of India's industrial policy was laid in the Industrial Policy Resolution (IPR) of 1948, which was revised in 1956 to incorporate the Mahalanobis strategy of growth and remained in vogue right up to 1991 with minor changes announced intermittently. Industries were divided into three broad categories: (1) "Schedule A," which included 17 industries, under five broad categories, defense industries, heavy industries, minerals, transport and communication, and power, reserved exclusively for public sector; (2) "Schedule B," which included 12 industries, sea transport, drugs, dyestuffs and plastics, fertilizer, synthetic rubber, chemical pulp, aluminum, etc., in which private sector firms would be accepted, although the public sector would play an increasing role in the future expansion of these industries; (3) all the remaining industries were open to private initiative subject to the Industries (Development and Regulation) Act of 1951. An industrial license was required to invest in capacity creation if investment or the value of equipment imports exceeded specified limits. The systems of industrial licensing and exchange controls were two major tools that the government used to make the private sector conform to the economic plans.

By the mid-1960s it was realized that the licensing system had done more harm than good to the cause of social justice because of corruption and politicization of the licensing decisions. The public sector had not been able to deliver the expected growth and could not generate internal surpluses for reinvestment even though a major share of investment in the five-year plans was appropriated by this sector. It failed to provide adequate supply of key services and inputs at reasonable cost due to inefficiency and waste in resource use, overmanning and mounting losses. Growth orientation received much more attention in actual implementation than the redistributive functions of the public sector during the Second and the Third Five Year Plan periods (1956–61 and 1961–66). It was realized that the benefits of economic growth had not trickled down to the poor, and that it was important to place greater emphasis on the social objective of poverty reduction.

India's industry went through three phases of growth during the period 1951–1991 period (see Krishna, 1997). There was a phase of rapid growth during 1951–1965 followed by a phase of deceleration during 1965–1980. The years 1980–1991 witnessed a revival of industrial growth. The most striking feature of Indian industrialization is the extent of diversification it achieved in a relatively short period from the mid-1950s to the mid-1960s. Self-reliance through the building of heavy industry was emphasized in the strategy formulated by Mahalanobis in the mid-1960s when India launched a major drive for industrial diversification. Steps were taken for the establishment of machine tools, heavy electricals, chemicals, machine building, and other heavy engineering industries.

The next fifteen years (1965–1980) turned out to be a phase of industrial deceleration. Whereas consumer goods and its main sub-category consumer nondurables experienced mild deceleration, heavy industry, consisting of basic and capital goods, suffered significant deceleration (Ahluwalia, 1985). In the use-based classification, the metal based category suffered marked deceleration. The major factors that seem to have contributed to the observed deceleration during the period 1965–1980 include: (1) slowdown in public investment and resulting inadequate infrastructure investment; (2) poor management of the infrastructure sector; (3) slow growth of agricultural incomes and resulting slow growth in demand for industrial products; and (4) restrictive industrial and foreign trade policies leading to high-cost industrial structure.

The industrial sector in India performed impressively in the 1980s (1980–1991) in terms of growth of output/value added compared to the period 1965–1980. The re-orientation of industrial and trade policies initiated since the mid-1970s received a fillip in 1985 with the introduction of some major policy reforms. However, Kelkar and Kumar (1990) have argued that the 1980s tended to give wrong signals, creating a bias in favor of chemical-based industries rather than metal-based industries in which the country had a comparative advantage. By relying on non-tariff forms of protection in conjunction with liberalized entry, the policy resulted in "excessive entry, high costs of production and lack of competitive quality in domestic industries."

2.1.3 Agriculture

India's development strategy since 1956 had a built-in "anti-agricultural" bias (see Gulati, 1998). This sector was implicitly "taxed" by trade policy even though there is very little incidence of direct taxation of agriculture. High protection for industry along with an over-valued exchange rate were the policy instruments that led to the implicit taxation of this sector. The assumption that growth in industry would provide jobs to the surplus labor force from the rural areas and hence improve productivity of the agricultural sector did not prove to be right. The share of agriculture in GDP has been declining much more rapidly compared with the decline in the share of labor force employed in this sector. The institutional reforms of agriculture in the form of land ceilings and tenurial reforms, undertaken during the first three five-year plans (1951–1965), did not lead to any significant improvement in the conditions of the small and poor farmers or in the productivity of this sector. It was the political economy of food shortage that led India into an era of technological upgrading of agriculture starting in the mid-1960s. The new agricultural strategy (Green Revolution) was based on high-yielding varieties (HYV) of seeds along with appropriate usage of irrigation, fertilizers and pesticides. The Agricultural Prices Commission (APC) was set up in 1965 as a permanent advisory body charged with the responsibility for developing a balanced and integrated price structure from the perspective of the overall needs of the economy and with due regard to the interests of producers and consumers. The body was renamed as the Commission for Agricultural Costs and Prices (CACP) in 1985. The final decision on agricultural prices remained with the government. The Food Corporation of India (FCI), also established in 1965, was expected to provide effective price support to the farmers. The price policy was combined with the operations of a public distribution system (PDS) to ensure the supply of foodgrains at subsidized prices to at least some of the poorer sections of the population. But the attention of the policy makers once again was shifted to industry after the world oil crisis of 1973–74. Since the 1980s, policy makers have made efforts to assist the industrial sector especially by means of input subsidies and price interventions. The anti-agriculture bias in the trade policy seems to have been partially taken care of after the trade policy reforms initiated in 1991, even though not much has been done to reform this sector as such.

The post-Green Revolution period up to 1991 may be divided into two distinct phases, 1967–68 to 1980–81 and 1980–81 to 1990–91. During the early phase, the major benefits of the new agricultural strategy remained limited to crops like wheat, regions of north-west India, and farmers who had access to the requisite credit. However, in the later phase, the benefits were spread to other crops like rice, pulses and oilseeds, whose growth rates during the first decade of the Green Revolution had fallen much below those recorded in the pre-Green Revolution period, to regions like western and eastern India which had been lagging during the early phase, as well as to the smaller farmers due to better credit availability during the later phase. While during the early phase of the Green Revolution, increase in yields per hectare accounted for as much as 80 percent of the increase in foodgrains output, the entire increase in output during the later phase is attributable to increase in yields.

2.1.4 Trade

India's foreign trade regime has undergone various changes during the 1951–1991 period (see Srinivasan, 1997). The First Phase of India's development experience, 1951–1965, involved three sub-periods. The 1951 to 1956 period coincided with the First Five Year Plan (1951–56) and was a period of good agricultural production and near equilibrium in the balance of payments. Quantitative restrictions (QRs) were not in much use. It was during the 1956–1962 period, which included the Second Five Year Plan (1956–61), that India entered into a phase of developing heavy industries. This led to a serious balance of payments crisis by 1957. The government opted for imposing QRs on imports rather than adopting appropriate macroeconomic policies, including exchange rate adjustment. Both the QR restrictions as well as the then existing industrial licensing policy were selective in favor of developing certain basic and heavy industries to encourage import substitution. The domestic import substituting industries were thus granted protection from foreign competition. The QR regime on imports initiated in 1957 was continued during the 1962–1966 period which was continued during the 1962–1966 period which roughly coincided with the Third Five Year Plan (1961–66). However, export subsidies were introduced in 1962 primarily to offset the disadvantage faced by exporters due to the QRs on imports. Foreign aid to India was suspended following the war with Pakistan in 1965. India faced a major drought in the 1965–66 agricultural year. This led to reduction in India's traditional exports as well as to the need for food imports. The bilateral and multilateral donors promised to resume aid to India on the condition of liberalization of the economy.

The second phase of India's development experience, 1965–1980, roughly coincided with three episodes of changes in foreign trade regime. The first subperiod of India's foreign trade regime was 1966–1968. India devalued the rupee by 57.5 percent in June 1966 along with elimination of export subsidies and reduction in import duties. According to Bhagwati and Srinivasan (1975), the total "net" devaluation on the trade account turned out to be 21.6 percent for exports and 42.3 percent for imports. The corresponding figures were 22.3 and 44.8 percent, respectively, on the current account. India faced another serious drought during 1966–67, which led to increases in prices. Traditional exports were even more adversely affected. Industry entered into a recessionary phase. The liberalization moves were abandoned by 1968 due to erosion of popular support for the Congress party in the general elections of 1967. Moreover, the promised foreign aid did not flow into the economy. The economy once again slipped back into a more restrictive trade regime during 1968–1975. There were several adverse exogenous shocks during this period. The Bangladesh war of 1971 was followed by poor agricultural performance during the adverse weather years of 1972–1975. Inflation reached double-digit levels during 1972–73 and 1973–74. India also had to adjust its economy to two international events in the form of collapse of the Bretton Woods system of fixed exchange rates in 1971 and the first oil shock in 1973. As foreign exchange became scarce, import policy became more restrictive and complex. The QR regime was made tighter. Tariffs were escalated to absorb partially the increasing import premia generated by the tighter QRs (see Rao, 1985). The economy entered subsequently into a more liberalized trade regime period during 1975–1985. Foreign exchange remittances from Indians working in West Asia registered a major increase. Agricultural production improved due to significant increases in the yield per hectare of wheat and the yield levels of rice also showed improvement. The slowdown in industrial activity as well as in public sector investment led to reduction in pressure on the balance of payments. Though imports of non-competing "essential" imports were liberalized, the domestic industry continued to enjoy complete protection from import competition.

The third phase of India's development experience (1980–1991) included half of the period of the liberalized trade regime of 1975–1985. The trade regime continued to be somewhat liberal during 1985–1991 even though the complex system of QRs remained in place. In 1985, a three-year import and export policy (1985–88) was introduced, followed by another three-year policy (1988–91). Though these policies were intended to provide some stability to the trade policy, the government nevertheless kept changing various aspects of the policy. Though a number of intermediate goods were taken out of QRs and put under open general license (OGL), many of these were non-competitive imports with no domestic substitutes. Furthermore, the goods put under OGL were subjected to high tariffs. Looking back at these experiences, it is now realized that import substitution and export promotion are neither mutually exclusive nor alternative strategies of development. Each of the two policies is important in its own right, and a healthy balance should be struck between them.

2.2 Major Features of the Indian Economy Towards the End of the 1980s[4]

2.2.1 The Emergence of Regulated Product Markets

As already mentioned, India entered into an era of ambitious industrialization during the mid-1950s with the Mahalanobis strategy of development as its basis. As in most other developing countries, export pessimism underlay India's development strategy. The basic emphasis was on import substitution, heavy industries, and a major role for the public sector. The government played a pivotal role in creating a highly regulated economic structure for the Indian economy. Different regulations and controls operated on trade, production, pricing, and distribution.

Trade Regulation

The trade policy regime was highly protectionist and regulated through quantitative controls on imports as well as exports. Tariff rates were exceptionally high. Domestic industry, heavily insulated from international competition, was under strict regulation. The two underlying assumptions were that the country would face a more or less permanent shortage of foreign exchange, and that the nascent industry could only be promoted through a protective foreign trade regime. It was believed that restricted imports would save foreign exchange and stimulate domestic output and innovation.

Production Regulation

The controls over production were introduced through the Industrial Policy Resolution (IPR) in 1956, and later through the Monopolies and Restrictive Trade Practices (MRTP) Act in 1969. The public sector was assigned an important role. The entry and growth of firms were subject to four sets of licensing policies: (1) capacity licensing; (2) monopoly control; (3) small-scale industry reservations; and (4) activities reserved for the public sector.

Capacity licensing was the instrument to be used to implement the planned growth of supply from different sectors to match the potential demand. However, this instrument was used by some of the large and influential industrial firms to forestall competition through filing counterfeit applications. The MRTP Act was introduced in 1969 to prevent the concentration of economic power and to curb restrictive trade practices. Firms with dominant market shares or having assets above a threshold limit were supposed to receive clearances before they could expand their production. The MRTP firms were generally restricted to core industries. These regulations restricted the growth of the large MRTP firms, thus possibly forestalling the benefits that could have been derived through economies of scale.

The attitude towards foreign direct investment (FDI) generally remained one of fear and suspicion until the early 1980s. Foreign collaborations were permitted only in areas in which India had not developed its capabilities. Therefore, India's policy towards FDI was quite restrictive and selective. It was only during the 1980s that the government relaxed its policy towards foreign collaborations. This was done specifically in respect of investors from Oil Exporting Developing countries.

Prior to 1991, the government was committed to enforcing the pace of indigenization in manufacturing. Local content requirements were forced on a number of engineering and electronic industries through "Phased Manufacturing Programmes" (PMPs). The government provided various concessions to the small-scale industrial sector mainly with a view to creating more employment. These included tax and interest rate concessions, some degree of assured government procurement, and reservation of a large number of items to be produced only in this sector. This forestalled competition from the large scale firms and also acted as an incentive for the "small" firms not to grow "large" lest they should lose the concessions they enjoyed. In general, the small firms were denied the benefits of economies of scale and suffered from technological obsolescence.

The public sector in India was expected to be the pinnacle of the economy through setting up and developing heavy industries (basic metals and capital goods) and infrastructure (power, transport, telecommunications, etc.). The expected investible surpluses were to be used for further development of the economy. However, the public sector grew in a haphazard manner and extended itself into non-core areas which were not part of the originally designed plan. The public sector was extended into areas such as tourism and hotels, and it took over struggling private industrial units through nationalization with a view to protecting employment (Ahluwalia, 1993). Huge subsidies were thus injected into the public sector to maintain and even expand its size despite the social costs involved.

Regulation of Prices and Distribution

Apart from industrial licensing and import controls, the government also attempted to control the prices and distribution of many commodities. The Ministry of Finance observed in a discussion paper on Administered Price Policy (1986) that: "The wholesale price index (WPI) consists of a total of 360 commodities of which there are 55 major items whose prices are either fully administered, partially administered or subjected to different forms of voluntary and other mechanisms of control. The total weight of these items in the WPI is 30.85 percent." The fully administered items included: petroleum products; coal; electricity; fertilizers; iron and steel products; nonferrous metals; drugs and medicines; and paper and newsprint. The items under dual pricing schemes (partially administered prices) included: rice; wheat; sugar; vanaspati (vegetable fat); and cement. The main objective of the administered price policy was to provide the poorer groups of the population with necessary consumer goods at low prices, to make certain crucial inputs required for the development process available at "right" prices, and to control inflation.

The government's methods of price and distribution control differed by industry and led to reduced profitability in such industries as steel, fertilizers, cement and foodgrains (paddy and wheat). In the case of the steel industry, most of the production came from public-sector plants. For a long time, the practice in this industry had been that a uniform price was paid to all plants, and the output was allocated to various users at a fixed price, with some users receiving a preferred treatment. In the case of fertilizers, different plants were paid different "retention prices," with higher prices to relatively inefficient plants so as to keep all plants operative. The pooled output, along with imports, was then distributed among users at a subsidized price so as to promote the usage of fertilizer. In the case of cement, a single plant received two different prices for the same product, with a "levy" quantity to be sold at a fixed price and the remaining quantity to be sold at the free market price. The "levy" cement was made available to priority users. The basic objective of price and distribution control in foodgrains was to make these available to low-income consumers at "cheap" prices and, at the same time, to ensure a "fair" return to the farmers. The government maintained buffer stocks of foodgrains that were built up through public procurement during the years of good crops and used to augment supply during the years of bad crops. Such operations also minimized price fluctuations. Nonetheless, the government had to foot a huge bill on account of subsidies provided to maintain these price and distribution controls.

The long-term consequences of India's restrictive industrial and trade policies started showing up by the mid-1970s. There was reduced domestic competition. Choice of plant size, changes in product lines, reductions in the workforce, selection of optimal locations, etc. were all quite limited. Many production units were using outdated technologies and were operating below minimum efficient scale. Costs of traded inputs were high. Exports could be competitive only through providing large subsidies and other incentives. Heavy protection to domestic industry discriminated against agriculture. Domestic industrial regulation, combined with high tariff walls and strict import licensing, resulted in a generally high-cost, inefficient industrial structure that was no match for world market standards in price and quality.

2.2.2 The Consequences and the New Policy Framework

The efficiency and growth of the Indian economy were modest by world standards during 1951–81 due largely to India's disappointing productivity performance. During the 1980s, growth momentum picked up somewhat, due partially perhaps to limited policy reforms that were introduced beginning in the late 1970s, but mainly due to increased borrowing and spending.

According to Bhagwati (1993), the two major elements of India's policy framework that had resulted in an adverse effect on the efficiency of the private sector were: (a) extensive bureaucratic control over production, investment and trade; and (b) inward-looking trade and foreign investment policies. In the case of the public sector, besides functioning inefficiently, it took upon itself the responsibility of entering into areas other than the conventional ones such as public utilities and infrastructure. The inefficiencies in India's policy framework, which had forced India to remain behind many other developing countries, had become evident by the 1980s. These inefficiencies were the cause of the Indian economy's failure to get adequate returns from its increasing investments. Apart from a defective policy framework, India's productivity had further been hampered by its failure to provide primary education to a large proportion of its population.

Beginning in the late 1970s, a process of industrial reforms began with some decontrol within a highly regulated policy regime. These reforms were aimed at domestic liberalization through a progressive shift from discretionary quantitative controls to nondiscretionary fiscal controls. The general emphasis was on introducing cost efficiency gradually, through domestic competition, without risking any sudden shocks. The important reforms in the area of industrial policy during the 1980s included relaxing licensing constraints on entry in priority sectors; growth (capacity re-endorsement); flexibility to respond to changing demand conditions (broad banding); and cost efficiency (prescribing minimum scales of production in a number of commodities). A comprehensive Industrial Policy Statement was announced by the Government in July 1980. The infrastructure sector (coal, power, and railways) received increased attention and emphasis during the 1980s. However, public sector reforms received much less attention than was required. Various official committees recommended the need to extend increasing autonomy to the public sector by distancing Government from it. It was only in the late 1980s that the Government introduced the so-called Memorandum of Understanding (MOU) that was designed to keep a public enterprise away from routine interference by its administrative ministry and to provide some degree of autonomy in its investment decisions.

A beginning was also made towards liberalization of India's trade policy regime during the late 1970s, and this liberalization gained some momentum during the latter half of the 1980s. The Committees led by P.C. Alexander (1978), Abid Hussain (1984) and Narasimham (1985) influenced Indian thinking on trade policy reform by emphasizing two major points: (1) on the export front, there was a need to develop an efficient system that would make exports less costly and more profitable; and (2) on the import front, there was a need to move away from a discretionary system of quantitative import controls to a system based on tariffs. The Long Term Fiscal Policy, announced in 1985, envisaged the eventual removal of import licensing from all imports except consumer goods and also proposed simplification of the complex tariff structure. Quantitative restrictions were in fact being gradually removed along with expansion in the open general license (OGL) list of imports. The imports of various capital goods and raw materials became freer as these were put on the OGL list along with reduction in their tariff rates. However, the changes that took place up to July 1991 were quite small by comparison to what was needed. The dominant view continued to be that if a good could be produced in India, then it should be protected from import competition irrespective of its cost of production. Thus, despite all these measures, the Indian economy remained a highly protected economy at the end of the 1980s.

2.2.3 The Degree of Protection Towards the End of the 1980s

A World Bank study (1989) estimated the nominal rates of protection (NRPs) for 56 major manufacturing sectors for the year 1986–87 based on comparisons of domestic and world prices of various commodities rather than on tariff rates. Its estimates of the effective rates of protection (ERP) indicated a bimodal type of protection. In terms of shares of gross value added, effective protection was "high" (above 70 percent) for 39 percent of manufacturing, "moderate" (30 to 70 percent) for about 6 percent, and "low" (less than 30 percent) for about 55 percent of manufacturing. The study found a positive relationship between protection and capital intensity. The industries enjoying high effective protection were relatively more capital and power intensive. Further, the employees of "high" protection sectors received relatively higher wages, whereas 78 percent of employment was in the "low" protection sectors. Thus, the study concluded that protection principally benefited capital intensive industries with a small minority of privileged workers. The measures of protection used in the World Bank study have the advantage that they incorporate the effects of tariff as well as non-tariff protective measures. The weighted average NRP was found to be 50 percent and the weighted average ERP, 40 percent, using value added at world prices as weights, and 46 percent using value added at domestic prices as weights.

In a study of protection and the industrial structure in India, Aksoy and Ettori (1992) concluded that the costs of production in various Indian industries had escalated as a result of the policy of high taxes and tariffs on capital goods and key intermediates during the pre-July 1991 period. Such a structure of protection led to much lower "net average protection" to the industrial sector as a whole. This study presented a comprehensive picture of the level of competitiveness of Indian industry in the late 1980s by computing around 500 price ratios between domestic ex-factory prices and cif import prices (nominal protection coefficients).

Based on about 210 ERPs taken from various sources and grouped into 16 product categories, the study further pointed out that the ERPs in Indian manufacturing showed wide inter-sector as well as intra-sector variations due to the combined effects of realized protection on inputs and outputs and the low value-added content of Indian industry (around 25 percent, on the average, in domestic prices). The generally high ERPs suggested that Indian industry had ample scope for earning profits and/or being inefficient. Relatively high effective protection was observed in: edible oils; heavy chemicals; iron and steel products; castings and forging; non-electrical machinery; electronics; synthetic fibers and resins; and synthetic textiles. The sectors with relatively low ERPs included: machine tools; hand tools; electrical machinery; motor vehicles and parts; cotton textiles; and aluminum products.

Despite various steps taken during the 1980s towards liberalizing India's trade policy, imports continued to remain highly protected. In fact, nominal and effective rates of protection (based on tariffs) for India's manufacturing sector appear to have increased over the 1980s (Goldar and Saleem, 1992). The weighted average NRP for the manufacturing sector (using value-added weights corresponding to 1983–84) increased from 91 in 1980–81, to 114 in 1983–84, and 122 in 1989–90.

Table 2.1 shows simple and import-weighted average tariff rates of six broad groups of products for the year 1989–90, based on the Tax Reforms Committee of the Government of India Report (1991). The simple average tariff rate of protection on agricultural products at 99 percent was much higher than the corresponding import weighted tariff rate at 46 percent. Cereals, pulses and rubber were the three major items of import. The duty rate for cereals was zero and very low for pulses. But the duty rates for rubber and other cash crops were very high, exceeding 100 percent in many cases. Thus, the simple average tariff rate for agricultural products turned out to be much higher than the corresponding import weighted average. This was the case also for other mineral products, though the import weighted average for this group was already relatively low. The weighted-average tariffs targeted for 1995–96 are shown in the last column of table 2.1.

TABLE 2.1. Average Tariff Rates for Broad Commodity Groups

Group	Weight (Import Based)	1989-90 Simple Average	Import Weighted Average	Target '95–96 Import Weighted Average
Agricultural Products	0.03	99	46	20
Coal, crude oil, & natural gas	0.16	82	54	34
Other mineral products	0.03	98	20	15
Manufactured products	0.78	123	98	49
Of which				
Consumer goods	0.07	138	89	60
Intermediate goods	0.47	125	103	45
Capital goods	0.24	94	91	55
Aggregate	1.00	121	87	45

Source: Tax Reforms Committee's Interim Report (1966, table 8.2, p. 104), Government of India.

Mohan (1992) used a different indicator to measure the competitiveness of the economy, based on actual duties collected as a proportion of actual imports. He contended that Indian industrial and trade policies were tightened after the mid-1960s, as this ratio was 18.2 percent on average during 1955–60 and 21.2 percent during 1960–65. But it started increasing thereafter to 28.5 percent in 1965–70, 34.2 percent in 1980–85, and 54.8 percent in 1985–90. More recent data indicate that this ratio was 50.4 percent in 1989–90 and then declined to 47.2 percent in 1990–91, 44.4 percent in 1991–92, 36.8 percent in 1992–93, 29.8 percent in 1993–94, and 29.2 percent in 1994–95.

The preceding discussion thus suggests that India had very sizable nominal and effective rates of protection through the end of the 1980s in many sectors. This is the case even though the precise estimates differ among the various studies noted because of the methods of measurement used and the particular years chosen.

It is important also to note that the rupee was continuously depreciating against the U.S. dollar prior to July 1991. The rupee exchange rate was Rs.12.20 per U.S. dollar in 1985–86, 17.90 in 1990–91, and 24.50 in 1991–92. The overvaluation of the rupee may thus at times have distorted some of the aforementioned tariff calculations.

2.2.4 Working of the Indian Factor Markets

Since, as already noted, the CGE model developed in the present study is intended to evaluate the comparative static effects of reforms in trade policy and certain domestic policy reforms on factor prices, economic welfare and the intersectoral allocation of resources, it is thus important to understand the salient features of the Indian markets both for factors of production (labor and capital) and goods. The speed at which adjustments take place in response to changes in macro- and microeconomic policies in an economy depends on price flexibility and on the speed and elasticity with which production changes in response to price changes. This, in turn, depends on the flexibility of real wages and the mobility of labor. Other important determinants of the speed of adjustment are responses to interest rates and movement of capital across different domestic sectors of production.

Indian Labor Markets

The "organized" sector in the context of the Indian economy consists of industrial establishments with 10 or more workers (or 20 or more workers if no power is used) and government services. It forms a very small proportion of the total labor force. The working population was about 298.7 million in 1990 (Economic Survey, 1995–96). Only 26.3 million persons were employed in the organized sector (both public and private), including 18.8 million in the public sector. The organized manufacturing sector (both public and private) employed only 6.3 million workers. Thus, only about 9 percent of total employment was "organized." Of the total organized sector employment of 26.3 million, nearly 71 percent was in the public sector and 29 percent in the private sector.

The process of structural re-adjustment of employment across the sectors of the economy is facilitated by wage flexibility in the labor market. This will depend on various regulations such as minimum wages, indexing, and direct determination of wages above any statutory minimum. The institutional intervention in the labor market through labor laws, other public regulations and trade unions also make the process of re-adjustment difficult. Except for the regulation of minimum wages, other regulations are applicable only to the organized sector which, as noted, is small in size. In the case of minimum wages, there is no national minimum wage and each state decides its own minimum wage for non-unionized sectors along with agriculture in some states. Despite its wide coverage, the minimum wage legislation is rarely enforced in the "unorganized" sector. Minimum wage legislation thus has little bearing on wage flexibility in India. Government regulation affects wage flexibility only in the small organized sector. The organized sectors are characterized by relatively more wage inflexibility than the unorganized ones because of the trade union power that is present. In the case of agricultural wage rates in India, it has been observed that real wages are flexible while the money wages are rigid downwards. The declines in real wages are generally associated with rising prices but not declines in money wages.

Indian Internal Capital Markets

There has been significant intervention by the government in the Indian capital markets since the 1950s. To begin with, the government wanted to reduce the role of unorganized moneylenders in the rural credit markets. Later, during the era of planned development, the government wanted to control the flow of funds through financial institutions to different sectors of industry. The interest rates in organized financial markets were administratively fixed. In some cases, the fix was on precise levels while in others there were ceilings and/or floors. This applied to the government's own borrowing and lending as well as to dealing by commercial banks and other financial institutions. The ceilings were prescribed even for corporate deposits, debentures and preference shares. Only the return on ordinary shares was not subject to any regulation. Thus, India has had a complex organized financial structure. In what follows, we consider only the most salient features of this financial structure.

The unorganized sector of the capital market in India operates through rural and urban moneylenders whose activities are outside direct government control. Reliable data for this sector of the capital market are not available. However, the unorganized sector of the capital market has been observed to follow changes in the degree of tightness of credit availability in the organized segment of the market.

The financial markets in an economy have two broad functional components: the money markets and the capital markets. The former deal in short-term funds while the latter deal in long-term funds. India has an established stock market for long-term corporate and government securities. It deals in new as well as old issues.

The Reserve Bank of India (RBI) is India's central bank and oversees the monetary as well as the financial system. Apart from performing the traditional central banking functions, the RBI has also undertaken since its inception a promotional role with a development orientation. It has played a dual role of building and strengthening India's financial infrastructure along with guiding and facilitating the allocation of a part of credit into socially desired directions.

Apart from promoting the spread of commercial banks, including regional rural banks throughout the country, the RBI has been instrumental in establishing, patronizing and promoting financial institutions that are expected to provide medium- and long-term finance to industry, mainly large industry. The main national level financial institutions for financing large industry are the Industrial Development Bank of India (IDBI), the Industrial Finance Corporation of India (IFCI) and the Industrial Credit and Investment Corporation of India (ICICI). The IDBI is the main institution for industrial development banking in the country. The financial needs of small-scale industries are taken care of by the Small Industries Development Bank of India (SIDBI). The corresponding institution for the agricultural sector is the National Bank for Agriculture and

Rural Development (NABARD). These institutions do not directly borrow from the public and obtain their resources instead from the RBI and/or other financial institutions.

Apart from these development banks, there arc non-bank financial institutions that provide long-term funds to industry, mainly in the form of shares and debentures. These are the Life Insurance Corporation of India (LIC), the four subsidiaries of the General Insurance Company (GIC) and the Unit Trust of India (UTI). These institutions directly mobilize savings by the public.

2.3 Economic Reforms in India Since July 1991

A program of macroeconomic stabilization was initiated by the government in July 1991. It consisted of reducing the fiscal deficit, controlling the money supply and correcting the overvalued exchange rate by a major devaluation of the rupee. The rupee was made partially convertible in 1992–93, fully convertible on trade account in 1993–94, and fully convertible on current account in 1994–95.

Apart from macroeconomic reforms, long overdue microeconomic or "sectoral" reforms with a medium term perspective were also launched. Major structural reforms were introduced in the industrial and trade policy regimes and in the financial sector with a view to improving the efficiency, productivity and international competitiveness of India's manufacturing sector. While significant changes in the industrial policy regime have led to industrial delicensing and a larger role for the private sector, the changes in trade policy involved abolishing import licensing except for imports of consumer goods. Reforms were also initiated towards streamlining the structure of indirect taxes and excise duties on domestically produced goods and custom duties on imports.

These unilateral reform measures along with reforms of the indirect tax regime represent a significant departure from the policy framework of the preceding four decades. They are consequently of crucial importance in influencing the future course of the Indian economy.

2.3.1 Trade Policy Reforms

With the trade policy reforms, various steps were taken to create a globally competitive environment by providing a stimulus to exports and reducing the degree of regulation and licensing control on foreign trade. As noted earlier, the rupee was devalued by about 20 percent in July 1991. A new system of incentives was introduced in July 1991 through the introduction of Eximscrips. Eximscrips were allotted to exporters as import entitlements against the value of exports. These scrips attracted a premium in the market and were freely tradable. In 1992, this system was replaced by a dual exchange rate mechanism under partial convertibility. Finally, the economy moved into a unified exchange rate system in 1993. The rupee has been made fully convertible on current account. The exchange rate of the rupee is now determined primarily by demand and supply conditions in the foreign exchange markets.

It is now widely accepted that these reforms have accelerated India's transition towards a globally oriented economy by stimulating exports and facilitating imports of essential inputs as well as capital goods.

One of the main objectives of the EXIM Policy was to phase out quantitative restrictions in the form of licensing and other discretionary controls. In 1991, imports were regulated by means of a positive list of freely importable items. Since 1992, imports have been regulated instead through a limited negative list. Import licensing controls have been virtually abolished except for the import of consumer goods. Almost all capital goods, raw materials, intermediates, etc. can now be freely imported subject only to payment of customs duties. In July 1991, 4,000 out of the 5,021 Harmonized System (HS) 6-digit tariff lines were subject to import licensing restrictions (Economic Survey, 1995–96). As of December 1995, more than 3,000 tariff lines covering raw materials, intermediates and capital goods are free of import licensing requirements. Further, another 1,487 tariff lines, whose import is otherwise restricted, are now allowed to be imported under freely tradable Special Import Licenses (SILs) which are granted to some of the export and trading houses based on the value of their exports.

Several steps were taken to stimulate exports. A system of value-based advance licenses was introduced. This permitted duty-free imports of necessary raw materials and components up to a stipulated percentage of the value of indicated exports. Self-certification advance licenses were made available for Export and Trading Houses, and these organizations have been permitted a larger range of imports while the scope of canalization (processing through public-sector undertaking) of both exports and imports has been narrowed. Established exporters have been permitted to maintain foreign currency accounts and to raise external credits to finance their trade transactions. The Export Promotion Capital Goods (EPCG) scheme was further liberalized to allow imports of capital goods at a concessional customs duty of 15 percent subject to an export commitment equivalent to four-times the CIF value of imports to be achieved over a period of five years. A zero customs duty may be levied for a seven-times export commitment. The Export Oriented Unit (EOU) and the Export Processing Zone (EPZ) schemes were liberalized and extended to agriculture, horticulture, aquaculture, poultry and animal husbandry.

The underlying philosophy of these trade policy reforms is based on the long recognized benefits that can be realized from the impacts that trade liberalization may have in enhancing the efficiency of resource allocation and consumer welfare.

2.3.2 Industrial Policy Reforms

With the industrial policy reforms launched in July 1991, licensing requirements were abolished for all except 18 industries (now reduced to 14). These industries were exempted because of their strategic and environmentally sensitive nature or their exceptionally high import content (see table 2.2). All other industries were permitted to expand according to their market needs without obtaining prior expansion or capacity clearance from the Indian Government. In the earlier licensing regime, the then existing manufacturers could produce only the licensed products. Now firms are free to manufacture any article (except for those subject to compulsory licensing) in response to market signals since industrial capacity licensing has been abolished.

TABLE 2.2. List of Industries Subject to Licensing

1.	Coal and Lignite
2.	Petroleum (other than crude) and its distillation products
3.	Distillation and brewing of alcoholic drinks
4.	Sugar
5.	Animal fats and oils
6.	Cigars and cigarettes of tobacco and manufactured tobacco substitutes
7.	Asbestos and asbestos-based products
8.	Plywood, decorative veneers, and other wood based products such as particle board, medium density fibre board, block board
9.	Raw hides and skins, leather and patent leather
10.	Paper and Newsprint except bagasse-based units
11.	Electronic aerospace and defense equipment; All types
12.	Industrial explosives, including detonating fuse, safety fuse, gun powder, nitrocellulose and matches
13.	Hazardous chemicals
14.	Drugs and Pharmaceuticals (according to Drug Policy)

Note: The compulsory licensing provisions would not apply with respect to the small-scale units taking up the manufacture of any of the above items reserved for exclusive manufacture in small-scale sector.

The need for separate permission needed by the firms covered under the 1969 Monopolistic and Restrictive Trade Practices Act (MRTP Act) for investment and expansion was also abolished. This was expected to encourage competition by reducing barriers to entry of new firms and to enable Indian firms to become large enough so that they could compete effectively in global markets. The amended MRTP Act gave more emphasis to prevention and control of monopolistic, restrictive and unfair trade practices so as to provide adequate protection to consumers.

The system of "Phased Manufacturing Programmes" (PMPs) was abolished. However, various incentives that were available to manufacturing units in 1991–92 through the then existing PMPs were to continue. The abolition of PMPs removed a major irritant in the form of government interference in business decisions.

Reforms were also initiated in public sector enterprises. In order to permit greater participation by the private sector in core and basic industries, the number of areas reserved for the public sector was reduced from 17 to 6. The six "reserved" areas are mainly those involving strategic and security concerns: defense products; atomic energy; coal and lignite; mineral oils; railway transport; and minerals specified in the schedule to the Atomic Energy Order of 1953. Some of the core industries that were reserved earlier are now open to the private sector, including: iron and steel; electricity; air transport; ship building; and heavy machinery industries such as telecommunication cables and instruments. It is expected that public enterprises will raise resources from the capital market on the strength of their own performance. Pressures on performance in the public sector are also mounting because the general economic environment is becoming more conducive to cost and quality considerations. The government has also attempted to disinvest shares of public sector undertakings in order to raise resources and encourage wider participation of the general public and workers in the ownership of these undertakings. The Committee on Disinvestment of Shares in Public Sector Enterprises (reconstituted by the Government in November 1992) chaired by C. Rangarajan made certain far reaching recommendations and suggested the setting up of a Standing Committee on Public Enterprises Disinvestment. It set the target of disinvestment in the public sector undertakings at 49 percent in industries reserved for the public sector and 74 percent in other cases. It remains to be seen, however, how much will actually be achieved.

The Government appointed Committee on Industrial Sickness and Corporate Restructuring submitted its report in July 1993. The Board for Industrial and Financial Reconstruction (BIFR), which was already dealing with private-sector units needing assistance, was entrusted with the responsibility to look after public-sector enterprises as well. Greater emphasis was given to improving performance of public sector undertakings through the instrument of Memorandum of Understanding (MOU) by which managements are granted greater autonomy and held accountable for results. The voluntary retirement scheme (VRS) was gradually being introduced in the public sector undertakings.

Reforms were also undertaken to encourage foreign investment and technology. The government has established a more liberalized foreign investment policy, which is in contrast to the previous policy of considering all foreign investment on a case-by-case basis and that too within the normal ceiling of 40 percent of total equity investment. The new policy provided for automatic approval of FDI up to 51 percent foreign equity holding in 35 specified high-priority, capital-intensive, high-technology industries, so long as the foreign equity covered the foreign exchange involved in importing capital goods, and outflows on account of dividend payments are balanced by export earnings over a period of 7 years from the commencement of production. Such equity participation has automatic approval and is cleared by the Reserve Bank of India. The procedures for investments in non-priority industries were also simplified. The Foreign Investment Promotion Board (FIPB) was set up to negotiate with large international firms and to expedite the clearances required. The Board was empowered to consider individual cases involving foreign equity participation over 51 percent. The Foreign Exchange Regulation Act of 1973 (FERA) was substantially liberalized to provide greater flexibility of operations to firms with foreign equity operating in India. Various restrictions on FERA companies were removed with regard to borrowing funds and raising deposits in India as well as taking over and creating any interest in business in Indian companies. The procedure for Indian business to operate abroad was also simplified. Indian companies and Indian nationals are now free to undertake joint ventures abroad as well as become directors in overseas companies. India has joined with many other developing nations to form the Multilateral Investment Guarantee Agency (MIGA) with an aim to promote foreign investment.

With these industrial policy reforms, India has moved into an era of a more competitive industrial environment in which entrepreneurs would be responding to the signals of the market rather than trying to skirt around bureaucratic controls. After a slowdown in industrial production during the first three years of the reform process, Indian industry witnessed robust growth of 8.6 percent in 1994–95 and 12.1 percent in 1995–96. The sale of shares of some public sector enterprises has introduced a new dimension into their strategic thinking with regard to profitability and long-term growth. Some public-sector undertakings are likely to approach capital markets directly to sell new equity. This should lead to a resource inflow into the public-sector undertakings. On the foreign investment front, the early results are encouraging, although it is too early to assess the actual inflow of investments. During the period August 1991 to March 1996, the Government approved 8,407 proposals for FDI and technical collaboration, with a proposed total investment of Rs.679 billion. However, the actual inflow of FDI during this period has only been Rs. 143 billion.

The National Renewal Fund (NRF) was set up in February 1992 to provide a mechanism for compensating workers in public sector enterprises subjected to restructuring. At the same time, the NRF is also expected to help restructure and modernize public-sector enterprises. The Department of Industrial Development administers the NRF. Its first activity involved cases relating to the National Textiles Corporation.

The small scale industrial (SSI) sector has an important role to play in the context of the labor-abundant and capital-scarce Indian economy. Various new policy measures for promoting and strengthening small, tiny and village enterprises were introduced in 1991–92. The major thrust of the new policy measures was to impart more vitality and growth to employment and exports. An Export Development Centre was established under the Small Industries Development Organisation. Industry-related services and business enterprises are now to be treated as small-scale units. The investment limit in plant and machinery of tiny enterprises was increased 2½-fold, irrespective of the location of the unit. In order to ensure adequate credit availability to the SSI sector, the eligibility limit of projects under the National Equity Fund Scheme was doubled for the project cost. The scheduled banks have been permitted to operate the Single Window Scheme in addition to State Financial Institutions.

The basic philosophy and common thread behind the various industrial policy reforms has been the resolve of the government to liberate Indian industry from the shackles of "controls" of various types. The "controls raj" had led to inefficiency and high-cost structure in Indian industry and corruption of various forms in the bureaucratic machinery responsible for "guiding and deciding" the path of industrial progress in India. The basic thrust has been to allow for more competition making free the entry of firms into different sectors of the economy. The realization that market forces can better look after India's industrial progress has ultimately dawned. It is better late than never.

2.3.3 Reforms in Indirect Taxes

With regard to tax reforms, steps were taken towards having a tax structure, encompassing both direct and indirect taxes, that is simple, that relies on moderate tax rates with a wider base and better enforcement, and that serves the purpose of equity. The tax structure was also expected to provide incentives and signals consistent with developing an internationally competitive and dynamic Indian economy. Direct tax rates were reduced. Customs duty reductions in combination with excise changes have put competitive downward pressure on domestic prices. The dispersion in excise duty rates has been reduced by bringing down higher end duty rates in particular and thus providing relief to consumers. In the present study, we shall mainly be concerned with the effects of restructuring indirect taxes.

The indirect taxes are distinguished as commodity taxes and other indirect taxes. Commodity taxes include union and state excise duties, sales taxes, customs duties (on imports and exports) and various other duties and taxes. "Other indirect taxes" include levies such as the electricity duty, motor vehicle tax, entertainment tax, stamp duty, etc. In practice, it is not possible to ascertain the exact amount of indirect taxes included in the value of commodities and services purchased by industries or final users since no information is available on the distribution of these taxes among different transaction flows.

In the case of the input-output table being used in the present study, the value of each of the indirect taxes as well as of subsidies for different sectors is apportioned in proportion to the value of the flow of commodities going to different industry sectors and final uses.

The Tax Reforms Committee (TRC), chaired by Raja J. Chelliah, has underlined the need for making the system of indirect taxation broadly neutral in relation to production and consumption, widening the tax base by covering exempted commodities and making a beginning with taxation of services. The modified value-added tax (MODVAT) scheme was introduced in 1986, mainly for reducing industrial costs and prices by relieving taxes on inputs, thereby mitigating the cascading effect on final products. Under the MODVAT scheme, a credit of duty is allowed on inputs that are used for producing excisable intermediate and finished products. The MODVAT scheme has undergone many changes, especially in the Budgets of 1994–95 and 1995–96. The major emphasis under indirect tax reforms has been on restructuring the excise duties. The ultimate objective of the reform of the Central excise system is to move towards a full fledged value-added tax (VAT) system at the Central level covering almost all commodities other than raw produce of agriculture and many, if not most, services. The Committee has suggested reduction in the multiplicity of rates of excise duties to 2 or 3 rates, at 10, 15 or 20 percent. A selective excise duty on non-essential commodities or commodities injurious to health could be levied at 30, 40 or 50 percent. Thus, the Committee has recommended a simple, broad based, indirect tax system that will have a few rates of duty at moderate levels, with the objective of moving towards a full fledged VAT for the commodities as well as the services sectors.

The other major area of reform, which was extensively discussed in the Tax Reforms Committee, relates to the structure of import duties. Prior to 1991, import duties were very high, touching a peak of 300 percent. A phased reduction in the peak rate of customs duty was undertaken in the successive Budgets to 150 percent in 1991, 110 percent in 1992, 85 percent in 1993, 65 percent in 1994, and 50 percent in 1995, with the exception of passenger baggage, alcoholic beverages, dried grapes, almonds and roller bearings. The import duty on capital goods for general projects and machinery, which was 85 percent prior to reforms, was brought down to 25 percent by 1995 and unified for nearly 80 percent of machinery. The customs duty on power projects and related machinery has been reduced to 20 percent and for fertilizer projects to nil. The number of duty rates has been reduced to 12 (including nil rate) at present. The Chelliah Committee Report (1991, 1992) had recommended the import-weighted average tariff rate for agricultural products be reduced from 46 percent in 1989–90 to 20 percent by 1995–96, but for other mineral products there was recommended a marginal decline from 20 to 15 percent only during the corresponding period. In the case of coal, crude oil and natural gas, the Committee had recommended a decline from 54 to 34 percent during the corresponding period, and for consumer goods, a decline from 89 to 60 percent.

The import-weighted tariff rates for intermediate and capital goods stood at 103 and 91 percent, respectively, in 1989–90, thus indicating that intermediate goods were more protected as compared to capital goods and consumer goods. This is an anomaly that needs to be corrected in the near future. The Chelliah Committee Report suggested rationalization of this tariff structure by bringing down the rate for intermediate goods to 45 percent as against 55 percent for capital goods by 1995–96.

2.3.4 Financial and Social Sector Reforms

The success of the ongoing process of economic reforms crucially depends upon the existence of an efficient financial sector, particularly the banking system, which is primarily responsible for mobilizing and allocating financial resources among different sectors of the economy. In order to achieve this objective, the Government embarked on a process of reforming the banking system and the capital market in November 1991, following the Narsimham Committee Report. The Government has now outlined the need and future guidelines towards reforming public sector commercial banks over a period of the next three years. The SLR and the CRR shall be reduced in stages so as to enhance the lending capacity of the commercial banks to various sectors of the economy on commercial considerations. The banks shall be required to follow internationally established objective accounting standards towards assessment and recovery of credit. In order to strengthen their financial position and to provide a basis for future growth, the banks shall be provided with additional capital from the Government and the capital markets. The banks shall be encouraged to adopt technological modernization along with enhanced managerial accountability and autonomy. The public-sector banks shall be encouraged to compete with the existing and the newly entering (though the entry would be controlled) efficient private-sector banks, including foreign banks. There is a proposal to create a new Board for Financial Supervision for ensuring compliance. The supply of credit to the rural sector, small scale industry and weaker sectors would be ensured through devising a viable mechanism.

Strengthening the social sector through development of human capital formation is important for an economy's rapid growth. India ranks at the 135th position according to the Human Development Index (HDI) reported for 174 countries (Human Development Report, 1996, UNDP). The HDI is a composite index of the levels of life expectancy, education and income in an economy. The adult literacy rate for India stood at 50.6 percent in 1993. Although India has a large pool of technical manpower, nonetheless the weak base of education among the Indian people may act as a drag on the future growth process.

It is well known that education has played a vital role in human capital formation in the East Asian economies. East Asia's success story is based on rapid accumulation of both physical and human capital. The governments of eight high-performing Asian economies (HPAEs) gave high priority to expanding primary and secondary education during the period 1965 to 1990 (World Bank Report, 1993). The HPAEs include Japan, Hong Kong, Singapore, Taiwan, Republic of Korea, Indonesia, Malaysia and Thailand. This resulted in stimulating the demand for higher education which has mainly been satisfied by the private sector.

Though India spent about 71 percent of its public education expenditure on basic education (primary and secondary) during the period 1987–90, the proportion of public expenditure allocated to education was only 8.5 percent during the period 1988–90. This was quite low compared to 22.4 percent of public expenditure allocated to education in the Republic of Korea during the corresponding period. The figure was 20 percent for Thailand, 18.3 percent for Malaysia and 15.9 percent for Hong Kong.

India needs to allocate more funds towards basic education, with relatively more emphasis on primary education and vocational education. Higher education needs to be more highly priced. Strengthening the primary education base would catalyze the process of economic growth in the country.

2.4 Concluding Remarks

The process of economic reforms in the Indian economy has completed more than six years of implementation, and the economy has attained a completely different profile compared to June 1991. However, on the macroeconomic front, the fiscal deficit still remains worrisome. While great progress has been made in reducing trade protection and enhancing industrial competitiveness, along with various tax policy reforms, a significant component of the structural reforms agenda still remains to be implemented. The process of economic reform has a long way to go in consolidating what has already been achieved (deepening of reforms) and, at the same time, extending its coverage to incorporate reforms in agriculture, the financial sector, taxation policies, infrastructure, labor laws, and the social sector pertaining to health and education (widening of reforms). If the policy makers are able to sustain and accelerate the process of reforms, a much brighter future seems to await India in the years to come.

CHAPTER 3

The India CGE Model of Production, Trade, and Employment

In this chapter, we outline the India computable general equilibrium (CGE) model that we have developed to evaluate the comparative static effects of selected trade and domestic policy reforms on output, trade, factor prices, economic welfare, and the inter-sectoral allocation of resources. The India model is a single country (versus rest-of-world) multi-sectoral CGE model. Though a single country model, the major source of inspiration has been the multi-country structure used in the Michigan Brown-Deardorff-Stern (BDS) CGE Trade Model (1996) and various research papers by the same authors.

3.1 Policy Relevance

India's unilateral trade and industrial policy reforms undertaken since July 1991 should be viewed in the context of the unilateral measures undertaken by many other developing countries in the past several years. Such policy changes will have medium- to longer-term impact on microeconomic or industry level variables within the individual countries along with re-alignment of production across countries of the world. It is therefore important to evaluate the economic effects of such policy reforms on factor prices, output, and trade, along with the inter-sectoral movement of resources, viz. land, labor and capital.

The issues that we will analyze have immense policy relevance for India. For example, policymakers need to know the likely direction of inter-sectoral changes that would result when India undertakes unilateral trade and industrial policy reforms. The industrial structure is expected to become aligned to the one that is internationally competitive. Thus, there may be a re-allocation of resources across sectors as a result of unilateral changes in trade policy. The analysis also provides estimates of likely changes in the sectoral composition of India's trade and how India's overall economic welfare will change.

3.2 Existing Models of the Indian Economy

Economy-wide empirical models have a long heritage in India. In the past, they have played a distinguished role both in terms of their impact on policy making and in generating better data for policy analysis. While models of various types ranging from planning models, econometric models to computable general equilibrium (CGE) models have been constructed over the years, there has been a distinct emphasis in India on econometric models.[5] Several reviews of Indian models are now available in Desai (1972), Jadhav (1990), Krishna, Krishnamurthy, Pandit and Sharma (1991), Marwah (1991) and more recently in Mallick and Kumar (1995). Consequently, we focus our attention on some important features of the various types of models developed in the past and their policy relevance. While our discussion covers all of the three types of models mentioned, our focus is primarily on the CGE models as they are hardly discussed in the other reviews.

Planning Models

The beginning of the planning process in independent India in the 1950s gave birth to a variety of planning models. Over the years, these models played a key role in the formulation of India's five-year plans. They have been useful to the planners for specifying the policies or instruments to achieve certain targets/goals as laid down in the five-year plans. However, the actual performance of all these models has been relatively poor in terms of the actual achievements of the plans compared to the targets that were set.

The earliest planning models in India were constructed by Mahalanobis (1953). He developed three models, namely, one-, two-, and four-sector models, of which the former two were used in the first and the second five-year plan formulations. All these models were inspired by Harrod-Domar growth models and are similar in nature. For example, the Mahalanobis two-sector model assumed that the economy consists of two closed sectors—consumption and investment—with different capital-output ratios. The model was a savings constrained model which recognized the rate of investment as the prime instrument for growth. However, the major weaknesses of the model were the absence of gestation lags between investment and production, exclusion of price effects, and the role of the external sector (Ray, 1989).

Sandee (1960) built a multi-sector optimization model based on India's 1953–54 input-output table. With this, the phase of aggregated planning models ended and multi-sectoral models came into being. The third five year plan formulation benefited from Sandee's model.

The fourth-plan period was influenced by the models of Chakravarty et al (1964, 1965). These were multi-sectoral optimization models, incorporating explicit inter-sectoral and inter-temporal relationships. Though the models were theoretically elegant, they abstracted from the reality of Indian conditions and especially ignored features peculiar to the Indian economy, such as the prevailing massive unemployment (Mallick and Kumar, 1995). During the same time, Manne and Rudra (1965) built a static, 30-sector consistency model that was used for generating terminal year projections for the fourth plan period.

The official Planning Commission model was introduced from the fifth plan period onwards. This model integrated a static input-output model (with 66 sectors), a growth model and a consumption model. The required level of investment for a set target for GDP was derived using aggregate incremental capital-output ratios (ICORs) and government consumption expenditures. Exports were exogenously specified while imports were projected based on past trends. The Input-Output system translated the final demand into sectoral outputs. The distinguishing feature of this model was the introduction of a consumption sub-model. This model for the first time addressed the issue of removal of poverty—the aggregate demand for consumer commodities was derived in a way that would ensure that basic minimum consumption needs of the bottom 30% of the population were met.

Subsequent planning models (viz., the sixth, seventh, and eighth plan models) retained the basic features of the fifth five-year plan model but made improvements with regard to the model size, detailed sub-models, use of improved econometric techniques for estimating consumption and investment (dynamic lag adjustment) relationships. The recently completed eighth five-year plan model is the most elaborate to date and includes a macro model, I-O model and an investment model at its core and six sub-models dealing with demography and employment, agriculture, industry, consumption, external trade and financial resources.

All these planning models suffer from a number of weaknesses such as exclusion of price effects, use of outdated I-O tables and omission of the spatial/regional aspect of planning.[6] Despite their limitations, planning models have attempted to give a direction to the development process of the Indian economy. They have been extremely useful in the solution of investment allocation and inter-sectoral consistency problems (Mallick and Kumar, 1995). But, under the post-1991 economic policy regime, the relevance of these models in their present form is marginalized, as the role of policy instruments in guiding investment decisions has become very limited.[7]

Econometric Models

Unlike the planning models, the econometric models in India have been primarily built by academicians in their individual capacities for forecasting future growth paths and understanding and assessing various short-run policy options vital to the state of the economy. Though the models have been largely built outside the policy-making framework of government, they have no doubt influenced government policies. The key characteristics of some of these models and their policy uses are shown in table 3.1.

TABLE 3.1. Main Characteristics of Econometric Models of India

	Study	Data base	Key Policy Uses and Results
1.	Marwah (1964)	1939–1960	Analysis of the effects of deficit financing for 3rd Plan under an assumed target growth rate of the economy. ***Results predicted accurately the inflationary impact of deficit financing.***
2.	Krishnamurthy (1964)	1948–49 to 1960–61	Predicting growth of national income over 3rd Plan.
3.	Ahluwalia (1979)	1951–1973	Effects of government policies with regard to public sector investment , current account expenditure on output and prices. ***Results show a tradeoff between output and prices.***
4.	Srivastava (1981)	1964–65 to 1974–75	Assess the impact of direct and indirect tax rates, restrictive monetary policy, increase in net foreign aid, etc. ***Results indicate that expenditure and deficit financing variables have a substantial impact on the system whereas changes in tax rates and liquidity ratios have marginal impact.*** Exploring the growth potential of the economy in the forecast period of five years under alternate policy options.
5.	Pani (1984)	1969–70 to 1981–82	Effects of increased sectoral investment by government, changes in administered prices on money supply and general price level. ***Results show that monetary theory of inflation does not hold well in the Indian context.***

6.	Krishnamurthy (1985)	1950–51 to 1979–80	Analysis of the relationship between inflation and growth and public and private investment ***Normal rainfall, increased availability of imported raw materials improve growth performance. Model results show that inflation is contained with monetary restraint, normal rainfall or decline in foreign inflation. Increase in real public sector investment raises economic activity along with crowding out of private investment.***
7.	Madhur (1987)	1951–52 to 1984–85	Analysis of fiscal and monetary policy changes. ***Increase in government investment financed by RBI borrowing improves output whereas same financed by commercial credit reduces output. Increase in money supply improves growth marginally at the cost of higher inflation.***
8.	Krishnamurthy, Pandit and Sharma (1989)	1960–61 to 1982–83	Implications of changes in rainfall, exports, and crowding out effects of public investment on economy. ***Results shows that enhanced absorption of infrastructural inputs improves overall economic performance significantly. Normal rainfall in subnormal years shifts growth path outwards for output, private investment and domestic savings.***
9.	Rangarajan and Arif (1990)	1961–62 to 1984–85	Effects of increase in government capital expenditure and sustained increases in money supply. ***Results suggest that higher capital expenditure increases output, but the increase in output and prices is dependent upon the extent of resource gap met through borrowings from RBI. The higher the dependence, the worse is the tradeoff between output and prices.***

(continued)

TABLE 3.1. *(Continued)*

10.	Rastogi (1991)	1950–51 to 1987–88	Simulating the effects of temporary/permanent changes on demand/supply side. ***Results indicate that effects on output generated by larger budget deficits are temporary and the GDP multiplier is less than unity.***
11.	Bhattacharya, Barman and Nag (1994)	1970–71 to 1990–91	Impact of stabilization policy measures on output, inflation, fiscal balance, foreign trade and domestic/external debt. ***Results indicate that success of stabilization programs is conditional upon weather conditions and improvement in productivity of capital and fiscal balance.***
12.	IEG-DSE Research team (1994)	1970–71 to 1990–91	Forecasting under alternate assumptions of rainfall, money supply and government investment.
13.	Joshi, Bhide, Kapoor and Satish (1995)	1970–71 to 1990–91	Forecasting and assessing the medium term impact of devaluation, poor rainfall and higher government investment. ***Forecasts of major macro variables are reasonably close to actual for the years 1991/92–93/94. Results suggest that higher government investment expenditure has most benefits in the long run. The impact of the bad rainfall scenario is lower in magnitude in the long run than short run.***

Inspired by the works of Klein and Tinbergen, econometric model building in India began in the early 1950s. Because of the lack of long time-series data and computing facilities, the early models were quite simplistic in nature. Of late (especially after the 1980s), more detailed models have been constructed. The earlier modelling work helped to clarify some of the modelling concerns in terms of specification of the economic relationships. In the later models, the new concerns of a more liberalized policy environment, with the opening up of trade and the financial sectors, are beginning to be addressed. However, all the models developed so far have been annual and country specific in nature. In this sense, the econometric modelling effort in India is still in a nascent stage.

Because the demand constraint was the focal theme of discussion in independent India, the early econometric models were developed in the Keynesian framework. The models by Marwah (1964) and Krishnamurthy (1964) may be mentioned in this connection. In her model, Marwah built a detailed endogenous price-determination mechanism. Price behavior was specified in two alternate forms, the quantity theory and excess demand. Aggregate demand equations, which were pivotal to price formation, were estimated in real terms. By contrast, the distinguishing features of Krishnamurthy's model were the endogenous determination of population and alternate specifications of economic relationships. The data base as well as the policy uses of these models are described in table 3.1.

The model by Pani (1977) deserves special mention. It is not only larger in size than any of its predecessors but also is the first model with a detailed treatment of the monetary sector.[8] Marwah rates this model as mild in elaborating the supply side, fair in analyzing the government sector, and extensive in its treatment of the monetary and financial sector. While modelling disaggregated investment behavior, constraints imposed by government activities, availability of domestic savings and inflow of foreign funds were recognized. Subsequently, Pani (1984) built another model with a focus on factors determining output, demand and prices. Similar to the earlier model, it has a fairly detailed treatment of the monetary sector with the money supply endogenous and linked to government deficits. The policy uses of this model are shown in table 3.1.

The dichotomy of the agricultural and non-agricultural sectors in the Indian economy is emphasized in Ahluwalia's (1979) model. A distinguishing feature of this model is its explicit treatment of the marketed surplus of foodgrains, which plays a key role in price determination. Price determination in her model follows an integrated approach rather than any particular theory of inflation, viz. Keynesian, monetarist or structuralist. The multiplier properties of this model are elaborated in greater detail than in any previous model.

In contrast to other models, Srivastava's model (1981) incorporated an explicit government budget constraint, an endogenous government consumption function and elaborate treatment of tax revenue functions. The other notable feature of his work is the interrelationship between the monetary and real sectors.

Several other models were also constructed in the 1980s and the 1990s as noted in table 3.1. Among them, only Pandit's (1986) and the IEG-DSE (1994) models contain a detailed treatment of trade and price formation.[9] However, one major weakness of the former model is that it ignores the monetary and fiscal aspects of the economy. The latter model is analytically more sound, its salient features including:

- decomposition of production, price formation and investment by five sectors;[10]
- decomposition of external trade to 1-digit SITC categories;
- endogenous determination of private capital formation;
- Cobb-Douglas specification for output determination with production relations being specified in productivity terms for both agricultural and non-agricultural sectors; and
- integrated approach to price formation.

The econometric model developed by Joshi, Bhide, Kapoor and Satish, (1995) at the National Council of Applied Economic Research (NCAER) is more detailed than any other existing models. A distinguishing feature of this model is the level of disaggregation in the manufacturing sector's output as well as in private final consumption expenditures,[11] while retaining the theoretical linkages between variables at a broader or more aggregate level. Thus, while the overall consumption level is linked to disposable income for the private sector, the sub-sector consumption expenditures are linked to relative prices as well. This model has been used for generating forecasts up to and beyond the year 2000.

CGE Models

Unlike the traditional econometric models, CGE models do not estimate but numerically calculate the model parameters (MacMohan, 1989). A CGE model is "computable" in the sense that an explicit numerical solution is calculated. The term "general equilibrium" refers to an analytical approach that views the economy as a complete system of interdependent components, such as industries, households, investors, government, importers and exporters (Dixon et al., 1992). Thus, in this class of models, supply/demand conditions in the factor and product markets are specified as functions of prices in a manner consistent with the optimizing behavior of firms and households. CGE models have been used quite frequently for policy analysis in developing countries, and several have been constructed for India, as noted in table 3.2. Since some of these models have been reviewed by Bandara (1991), we focus our attention mostly on more recent models.

The intricacy of India's agricultural pricing policies and its impact on income distribution have been a topic of discussion in the 1980s (Quizon and Binswanger (1986)). Consequently, three models constructed in the 1980s, viz. DeJanvry and Rao (1986), Narayana, Parikh, and Srinivasan (1991), and Subramanian (1993), have attempted to look at these issues. A special feature of the DeJanvry and Rao model is that it explicitly modeled government expenditure and revenue, making it possible to study the budgetary implications of such policy instruments as price supports, minimum wages, procurement of crops and food subsidies.

The model by Narayana, Parikh and Srinivasan is a class apart from the other CGE models in the sense that most of the parameters of the model are econometrically estimated.[12] The model has a detailed agricultural sector and is monetarily neutral. This model was built with a view to explore policy initiatives that promote growth and structural transformation while ensuring social justice.

By contrast, Subramanian (1993) combines the multi-market approach to modelling agricultural supply and input demand with the traditional CGE approach for other sectors, thus permitting explicit modelling of substitution between crops. His model consists of 17 commodity sectors with econometrically estimated supply functions for major crops. It also assumes product differentiation between imports and domestic production and exports and domestic sales and incorporates trade quotas in some sectors.[13] Wages adjust partially to food prices in the medium run and are determined by market clearing in the long run. Another special feature of this model is the determination of a rice and wheat procurement function through econometrically estimated equations where procurement prices are expressed as a linear function of output and the ratio of the procurement to the open-market price.

In contrast to other CGE models, the works by Rattso (1987, 1988) focus on the macrodynamic aspects of the economy. He draws upon the static structuralist macro model for India developed by Lance Taylor at MIT and a closed Leontief model built at the NCAER (Sarkar and Subbarao, 1981). Although there are no simultaneous estimations of the equations of the static part of the model, some coefficients are based on econometric estimation. The dynamic features of the model include investment response in agriculture and manufacturing and wage indexation. The main dynamic adjustment mechanism is related to capital accumulation. Terms of trade and public investment in agriculture determine private investment in agriculture whereas private investment in non-agriculture is determined by real sectoral profits in terms of investment goods and public investment. The accumulation of capital stock in

TABLE 3.2. Main Characteristics of Selected CGE Models of India

	Author and Data	Key Structure	Key Policy Uses and Results
1.	Sarkar and Rao (1981) Data: Mainly 1978/79 SAM Base year: 1978/79	Supply side: Not specified Demand side: LES Demand system	Analysis of short-term macro adjustment policies on deficits, inflation and balance of payments.
2.	Gupta (1983) Data: I-O table. All parameter values are obtained from empirical studies. Base year: 1979/80	Supply side: Nested Production function (Leontief, CRESH, CES) Demand side: Additive utility function with CES nests. Houthakker-Sato expenditure system used	Effect of 100% increase in oil price in short run and medium run. ***Short-run results show that the composition of industrial structure moves away from traded to non-traded goods and a fall in GDP. The worst effects on GDP can be reduced in the medium run.***
3.	Gupta and Togan (1984) Data: Mainly I-O table	Supply side: Nested Production function (Leontief, CES and CRESH) Demand side: LES Demand System	Effects on income distribution: -intervention (fixed wage and exchange rate) -semi-intervention (without fixed real wage) -semi-liberalized (without fixed exchange rate -liberal (with 10% cut in import tariff) ***In terms of GDP, the last policy measure is superior to others. It especially benefits peasants and non-agricultural workers.***

4.	Cole and Meagher (1984) Data: 1968/69 SAM Base year: 1968/69	Supply side: Fixed Coefficients Demand side: Fixed Coefficients	Effects of various redistribution policies considering two-way relation between growth and income distribution. ***Growth may give rise to significant shift in the distribution of income depending on whether or not it alters the relative scarcity of factors of production.***
5.	Narayana et al (1987) Data: Parameters related to demand and supply functions econometrically estimated Base year: 1980	Supply side: Not specified Demand side: LES Demand system	Effects of four polices of food-grains purchasing and subsidized distribution to consumers. ***Results show that income distribution improves under procuring and freely distributing 100 kg of grain per capita per year and financing costs through additional taxation with no fall in growth.*** Effects of four foreign trade and aid policies. ***Results show that there is no presumption that liberalization improves social welfare. Increase in aid improves social welfare in urban areas and worsens it in rural areas.***
6.	DeJanvry and Rao (1986) Data: Mainly 1977–78 SAM	Supply side: Not specified Demand side: LES Demand system	Simulates the income distribution, sectoral growth effects and budgetary implications of the following economic policies: (1) price support interventions; (2) price incentives to supply response; (3) food subsidy programs; (4) technological and irrigation programs. ***Public investment in technology and critical infrastructure for agriculture has more benefits in the long run than any other alternative policies.***

(continued)

TABLE 3.2. *(Continued)*

7.	Rattso (1988) Data: 1980/81 SAM and national accounts of 1980/81 to 1984/85 Base year: 1980/81	Supply side: Not specified Demand side: LES Demand system	Analysis of expansionary fiscal policy, shift in investment strategy of government, and increase in private agricultural investment. ***Results show that reallocation of investment in favor of agriculture affects overall economic performance and lowers inflation. An increase in agricultural investment alone stimulates growth rate with inflationary pressure.***
8.	Pradhan, et al (1990) Data: Parameters estimated using time series data for the period 1960/61–1980/81. Base year: 1980/81	Supply side: Estimated equation Demand side: LES Demand system for some sectors, and in others estimated equation	Analysis of complementarity between public and private investment under different modes of allocation and financing public investment. ***Results show that although public investment crowds out private investment, it promotes growth.***
9.	Sarkar and Panda (1989, 1990, 1991) Data: Mainly 1985/86 SAM Base year: 1985/86	Supply side: Not specified Demand side: LES Demand system for household and Leontief type demand-determined output level	Forecasting and policy simulations relating to agricultural output and prices, investment under alternate modes of financing, resource mobilization through various instruments, changes in exchange rate, energy price, and fiscal deficit reduction. ***The overall effect of fiscal squeeze is generally recessionary and deflationary. Also model results reveal the interdependence among instruments of fiscal squeeze. The effect of devaluation is always inflationary. The trade deficit improves only if trade elasticity is more than 0.8. The overall demand effect of food price decrease is recessionary except for foodgrains whose consumption increases.***

10.	Narayana, Parikh and Srinivasan (1991) Data: Parameters empirically estimated from time series data.	Supply side: Estimated eq. Demand side: Consumer behavior characterized by separate expenditure system.	Analysis of impact of policies relating to public distribution, foreign trade, irrigation development, rural works programs and agriculture/industry terms of trade. ***In stimulating agricultural growth, the development of irrigation and new varieties play a more important role than output pricing and input subsidy. Rural works program is an attractive program for improving the income of the rural poor.***
11.	Subramanian (1993) Data: Mainly 1983/84 SAM	Supply side: Based on normalized quadratic profit function for agriculture and traditional CES production approach for other sectors. Demand side: LES Demand system	Effects of changes in world economic environment and domestic policy reforms. ***Policies aimed at industry are more important to agriculture than agricultural specific policies. Further, study concludes that measures like targeted food subsidy may be necessary to offset adverse effects of liberalization.***
12.	Storm (1995) Data: Mainly 1985/86 SAM		Policy experiments relating to changes in government investment in agriculture, food-grains distribution, procurement prices, and fertilizer subsidy ***Results shows higher growth potential of expenditure on irrigation than on fertilizer subsidy and agricultural prices.***

(continued)

TABLE 3.2. *(Continued)*

13.	Bhide and Pohit (1993) Data: Mainly 1985/86 SAM Base year: 1989/90	Supply side: Not specified Demand side: LES Demand system for households and estimated export demand functions	Policy simulations relating to money-price linkages, exchange rate and changes in indirect tax rate. ***Currency depreciation/higher export elasticities lead to an improvement in trade/current account deficit at cost of lower growth and higher inflation. Reduction in tax rate leads to higher growth, lower inflation at the cost of higher budget deficit.***
14.	Bhide, Panda, Pohit and Joshi (1994) Data: Mainly 1989/90 SAM Base year: 1989/90	Supply side: Partly specified Demand side: LES Demand system for households	Examination of selected alternatives relating to Indian government's fertilizer pricing polices. ***Increase in administered prices of fertilizer leads to lower GDP, budget deficit and a higher price level. The impact worsens significantly under price decontrol scenario despite sharper fall in budget deficit.***
15.	Bhide, Sinha, Pohit and Joshi (1995) Data: Mainly 1989/90 SAM Base year: 1989/90	Supply side: Partly specified Demand side: LES Demand system for households, and estimated equations for trade.	Short-term forecasting and various policy experiments relating to changes in tax rates, exchange rates, investment expenditures, and interest rates. ***Results indicate that a policy mix to offset short-term adverse growth and price impact appears to be optimal.***

agriculture determines the actual production, and in non-agriculture it augments the production capacity.

The formulation of the structuralist macroeconomic theory by Taylor (1983) has inspired a series of structuralist CGE modeling efforts at the NCAER in India. The earliest model in this tradition is documented in Sarkar and Subbarao (1981). This was a three sector CGE model built around the consistency framework of a Social Accounting Matrix (SAM). Since then, a number of modifications have been made in the model, and it has been continuously used for policy simulations and short-term forecasting for over a decade now. Improvements in the model have been made from time to time and various versions of the model have been reported in Sarkar and Panda (1989), Panda and Sarkar(1990, 1991), Bhide and Pohit (1993) Bhide, Panda, Pohit and Joshi (1994), and Bhide, Sinha, Pohit and Joshi (1995). Table 3.2 documents the various changes/improvements that the NCAER model has undergone.

3.3 CGE Models: Conceptual Issues

The "computable general equilibrium" (CGE) modelling approach is an empirical counterpart of general equilibrium analysis. The term "general equilibrium" refers to an analytical approach which views the economy as a complete system of interdependent components, such as industries, households, investors, government, importers and exporters (Dixon et al., 1992). The term "applied" general equilibrium (AGE) models is also often used.

Whereas a partial equilibrium approach may be preferred due to its analytical simplicity, the reliability of the results increases considerably by using a general equilibrium approach (Whalley, 1975). Hence, in the CGE approach, the emphasis is put on numerical solution rather than obtaining formal analytical proofs of the existence and the uniqueness of equilibrium as in formal theoretical general equilibrium analysis (Bandara, 1991). In the CGE framework, the main focus of the analysis is quantitative and is based on empirical data from the particular country or group of countries being investigated. This enables one to obtain more useful information for analyzing the policy variables than is otherwise possible. Thus, CGE models are convenient tools for investigating the potential impacts of various economic policy changes on microeconomic and structural variables in an economy.[14]

Many CGE model exercises have been devoted to the impact of changes in policies related to international trade by a single country or a group of countries. For example, it is possible to compute the potential effects of a proposed or actual cut in tariffs on employment and output across different sectors in the individual economies and groups of economies. There will be a change in the consumption patterns due to changes in the relative prices of imports and domestic goods. This will induce changes in allocation of resources in the country. Such a chain of events cannot be captured readily by partial equilibrium models. CGE models are therefore more suitable for the purpose.

3.4 The Distinguishing Features of the India CGE Model

The CGE model that has been developed in the present study is distinctly different from the existing models of the Indian economy. It is a single country (versus rest-of-world, ROW) model and is capable of evaluating the comparative static effects of selected trade and domestic policy reforms on output, trade, factor prices, economic welfare and the inter-sectoral allocation of resources across 34 sectors of the economy. It also permits calculation of the aggregate impacts. The major source of inspiration in developing this model has been the multi-country structure used in the Michigan CGE Model by Brown, Deardorff, and Stern (1996) and various other research papers by the same authors (see references). The equations and technical details of the model are presented in appendix 1 below.

Our India CGE Model has various departures from the assumptions of the standard Heckscher-Ohlin (H-O) Model of international trade. It incorporates several of the assumptions of the New Trade Theory such as particular forms of increasing returns to scale, product differentiation and imperfect competition, none of which is permitted in the H-O Model.

The agricultural and service sectors in India are characterized in the model as being perfectly competitive, although the paddy (rice) and wheat sectors are modeled under an administered price regime. The product of each of these sectors is homogeneous but differentiated from imports. This assumption of national product differentiation is commonly known as the Armington assumption. These two sectors are modeled with constant returns to scale. The rail transport sector is modeled as a state monopoly sector.

The manufacturing sectors are characterized as being monopolistically competitive with free entry, and the products that are produced and traded are assumed to be differentiated by firm. Product differentiation by firm dispenses with the Armington assumption, so that the potentially strong terms-of-trade effects associated with national monopoly power are greatly diminished. Varieties enter via a Dixit-Stiglitz (1977) aggregation function into both utility and production functions, with implications that greater variety reduces cost and increases utility. However, some of the manufacturing sectors in India are state monopolies. The prices in these sectors are administered and products may be considered to be homogeneous only to be differentiated from imports. The same holds true of three private sectors in which the prices are administered. These are paper products, fertilizer and nonferrous metals. Except for the state monopolies and sectors with administered prices, the remaining manufacturing sectors are modeled with increasing returns to scale.

3.5 Model Implementation

The reference year of the model is 1989–90. The trade policy inputs into the model are the tariffs and NTBs that were applicable to India's trade in 1989–90. In order to investigate the sectoral employment effects of the unilateral trade liberalization, it has been assumed that the existing bilateral tariffs will be removed and NTBs relaxed in two stages, the first stage to be completed by the mid-1990s and the second towards the end of 1990s.

The domestic policy inputs include reduction in "other net indirect taxes" (indirect taxes net of custom duty and subsidies) and changes in administered prices in the regulated sectors. Since July 1991, there has been an effort to reduce indirect taxes and to increase the administered prices of paddy and wheat.

When policy changes are introduced into the model, its solution yields percentage changes in sectoral employment and certain other variables of interest for India. Multiplying the percentage changes by actual (1989–90) levels given in the data base yields the absolute changes, positive or negative, that might result from the unilateral trade and domestic policy reforms that have been undertaken.

In addition to the sectoral effects which are the primary focus of our analysis, the model also yields results for changes in total exports, total imports, the terms of trade, the overall level of welfare in the economy, and the economy-wide changes in real wages and returns to capital. Because both labor and capital are assumed to be homogeneous and intersectorally mobile in these scenarios, we cannot distinguish effects on factor prices by sector. Nor can we distinguish effects on different skill groups or other categories of labor. In particular we are unable to address the important question of how trade liberalization might affect the differential between the wages of skilled and unskilled workers.

In our model, we do not distinguish consumption from other forms of final demand. It is also assumed that aggregate expenditure varies endogenously to hold aggregate employment constant. Such a closure may be thought of as analogous to the Johansen closure rule (Deardorff and Stern, 1990). The Johansen closure rule consists of keeping the requirement of full employment while dropping the consumption function. This means that consumption can be thought of as adjusting endogenously to ensure full employment. However, in the present model, we do not distinguish consumption from other forms of final demand. That is, our assumption is that expenditure adjusts to maintain full employment. This may be thought of as analogous to the Johansen closure rule. This assumption is made so as to abstract from macroeconomic forces and focus on the intersectoral allocation of resources.

3.6 Documentation of the India CGE Model

India is modelled to produce, consume and trade 33 tradable goods. In addition, there is one non-traded sector, rail transport. The sectoral breakdown, as shown in table 3.3, has been concorded from ISIC Rev.2. Table A.1 in appendix 1 provides a key to the sectoral classification into different sets and subsets. Table A.2 is an extension of table A.1 to facilitate a better understanding of the sectoral classification.

The market structure in 29 of the 34 sectors is either perfectly competitive or monopolistically competitive, depending on the assumed degree of scale economies in production. The remaining 5 sectors are assumed to be state monopolies (SMS), including rail transport, which is the only non-traded sector, petroleum products, iron and steel, mining and quarrying, and electricity, gas, and water supply. Out of 33 tradable sectors, 9 are assumed to be under perfect competition (TPCS) and 4 under state monopolies (TMCS). The remaining 20 sectors are assumed to be under monopolistic competition (TICS), although there are three sectors in which prices are administered (TICSAP).

The final consumer demand equations for all sectors are obtained assuming a representative consumer who maximizes utility subject to a budget constraint. The revenues from tariffs and indirect taxes along with profits of the state monopoly sectors are assumed to be redistributed to consumers and spent. Intermediate demands are derived from the profit-maximizing decisions of the representative firms in each sector.

Consumers and producers are assumed to use a two-stage procedure to allocate expenditure across differentiated products. Consumer behavior is depicted in figure 3.1 and producer behavior in figure 3.2. At the first stage, expenditure is allocated across goods without regard for the country of origin (whether India or ROW) or the producing firm. At this stage, the utility function is taken to be Cobb-Douglas. The production function in each sector at this stage requires inputs in fixed proportions. In the second stage, final expenditure by consumers and expenditure on intermediate inputs by producers are both allocated (identically) within each sector in ways that depend on the sector's industrial structure. Expenditure on monopolistically competitive goods is allocated across competing firms in India and ROW. In the case of perfectly competitive goods, individual firm supply is indeterminate. Therefore, expenditure on each sector is allocated between the domestic industry as a whole and imports from ROW. The aggregation function in the second stage is a Constant Elasticity of Substitution (CES) function.

TABLE 3.3. Sectoral Breakdown of India CGE Model

Sector Number	Sector	ISIC Code
1.	Paddy	1A
2.	Wheat	1B
3.	Other cereals	1C
4.	Other agriculture	1D
5.	Food, Beverages, Tobacco	310
6.	Textiles	321
7.	Clothing	322
8.	Leather products	323
9.	Footwear	324
10.	Wood products	331
11.	Furniture and Fixtures	332
12.	Paper and Paper products	341
13.	Printing and Publishing	342
14.	Fertilizer	35A
15.	Other chemicals	35B
16.	Petroleum and related products	35C
17.	Rubber products	355
18.	Nonmetallic mineral production	36A
19.	Glass and Glass products	362
20.	Iron and Steel	371
21.	Nonferrous metals	372
22.	Metal products	381
23.	Nonelectric machinery	382
24.	Electric machinery	383
25.	Transport equipment	384
26.	Miscellaneous Manufactures	38A
27.	Mining & Quarrying	2
28.	Electricity, gas & water supply	4
29.	Construction	5
30.	Wholesale Trade	6
31.	Rail transport	7A
32.	Other transport, storage and Communication	7B
33.	Financial Services	8
34.	Personal Services	9

Note: ISIC codes are as per Rev. 2.

Figure 3.1. Consumer Behavior (Utility Maximizer, Two Stages)

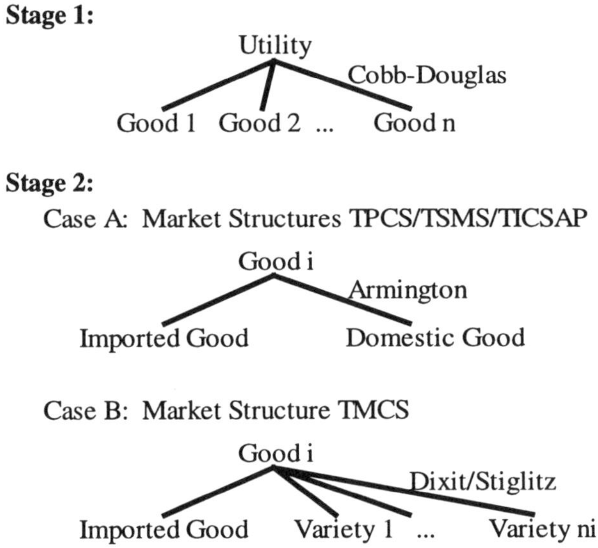

In the case of factor markets, the variable input requirements are taken to be the same for the three market structures. Primary and intermediate input aggregates are required in fixed proportion to output. Expenditures on primary inputs are allocated between capital and labor, assuming that a CES function is used to form the primary inputs aggregate. In the case of four agricultural sectors, land (along with capital and labor) is also assumed to be one of the primary factors of production. The primary inputs aggregate in these cases is a CES function of labor and a composite of land and capital. The composite of land and capital is in turn also a CES function. In the monopolistically competitive sectors as well as in the state monopoly sectors, additional fixed (independent of output) inputs of capital and labor are required. It is assumed that fixed capital and fixed labor are used in the same proportion as variable capital and variable labor so that production functions are homothetic. Capital and labor are assumed to be perfectly mobile across sectors except that all capital is assumed to be immobile into and out of the state monopoly sectors. However, we keep the option of specifying sector-specific

Figure 3.2. Producer Behavior
(Cost Minimizer, Two Stages)

Stage 1:

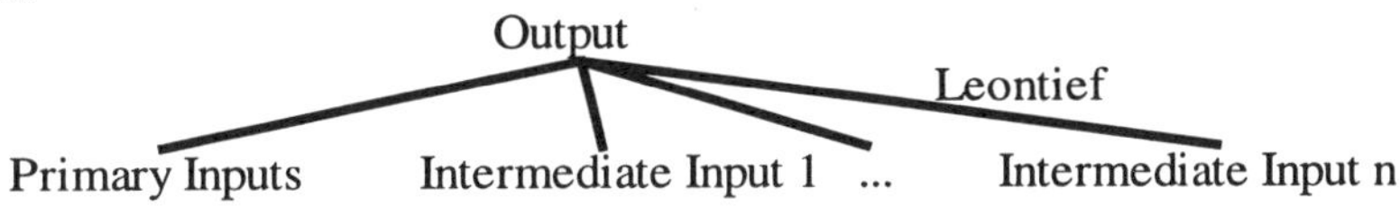

Stage 2 - Primary Inputs:

Case A: All Except Agriculture

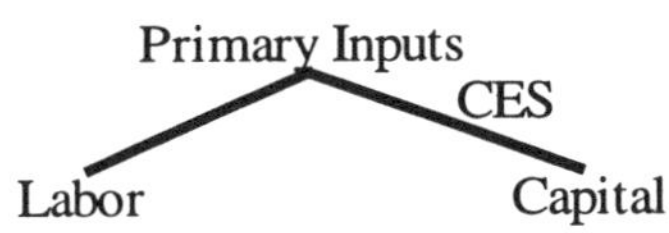

Case B: Agriculture (TAGS)

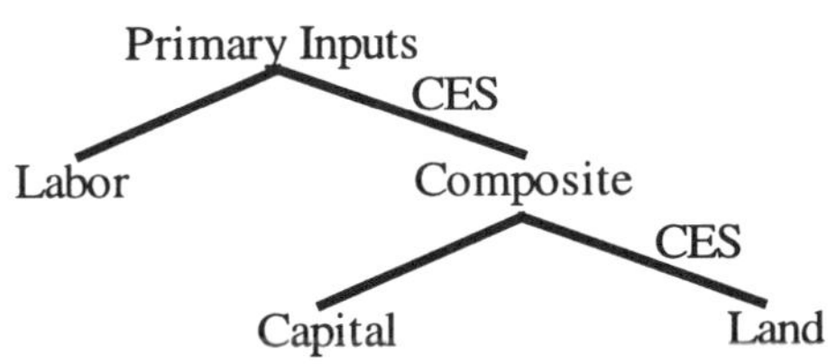

Stage 2 - Intermediate Inputs:

Same as Consumer Stage 2. See Figure 3.1

capital in other sectors also for some purposes, especially for short-term analysis. Land usage in agriculture is assumed to be substitutable across the four agricultural sectors. Returns to land, capital (in sectors across which it is mobile) and labor are determined to equate factor demand to an exogenous supply of each factor. The aggregate supplies of labor, capital and agricultural land are assumed to remain fixed (see figure 3.3).

Perfectly competitive firms set price equal to marginal cost, while monopolistically competitive firms maximize profits by setting price as an optimal markup over marginal cost. The numbers of firms in sectors under monopolistic competition are determined by the condition that there are zero profits.

Figure 3.3. Factor Markets
(Full Employment of Resources)

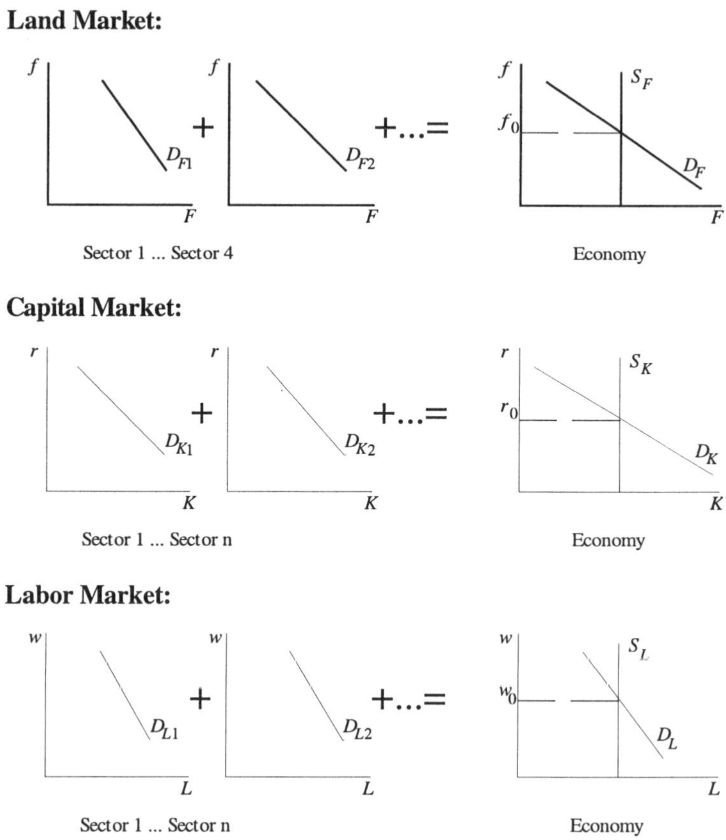

The numbers of firms in the state monopoly sectors as well as in the three administered price sectors under imperfect competition are assumed to remain fixed. The profits in these sectors are assumed to be redistributed to be spent on consumption.

International trade in goods by India is assumed to be subject to tariffs and NTBs. NTBs are incorporated as in Deardorff and Stern (1986, pp. 21-22) by endogenously solving for the ad valorem tariff-equivalent rate that would hold imports within each product category covered by NTBs at a predetermined level. An ad valorem tariff variable in each product category is then an average of this NTB tariff-equivalent rate and the nominal tariff rate, using the NTB coverage ratio to weight the NTB tariff equivalent. Tariff rates are aggregated according to the sectors specified in this model.

In the nontradable rail transport sector, total demand must equal national output. The price received by suppliers in this sector is assumed to be set by the government and hence is exogenous. Demanders pay an endogenous premium that equates demand to supply. For two of the four agricultural sectors, viz. other cereals and rest of agriculture (which are under perfect competition), prices adjust so that total demand (inclusive of exports) for the sector's product equals its output. In the case of the remaining two agricultural sectors, paddy and wheat, as well as in four tradable state monopoly sectors, the prices are assumed to be administered by the government. In three of the sectors under imperfect competition, viz. paper products, fertilizers and non-ferrous metals, the prices have also been assumed to be administered.

When analyzing the impact of reforms on the economy, we run two different sets of simulations. The first set of simulations is run while retaining the product market restrictions mentioned above. The second set is run after relaxing these product market restrictions. It is then assumed that none of the sectors is a state monopoly and that prices are not administered in any of the sectors.

CHAPTER 4

Implementation of the Model

4.1 Introduction

In the preceding chapter and in appendix 1, we have presented our model as a system of simultaneous linear equations incorporating economic variables and parameters. In designing the model, our objective was to take into account as many as possible of the interconnections among industries at the microeconomic level. This enables us to examine a variety of economic issues that most other existing models of the Indian economy cannot address, either because they are too highly aggregated, or because they are specified only in partial equilibrium terms. By the same logic, our model is too large to be able to say anything concrete without further specification of the parameters. Moreover, the level of disaggregation in our model implies an immense amount of effort to generate these parameters. To deal with this, we have relied, whenever necessary, on parameter estimates already available in the literature.

The chapter proceeds as follows. In Section 4.2, we discuss the data and parameters of the model. The solution procedure of the model is discussed in Section 4.3. Finally, Section 4.4 reports results of the model.

4.2. Data and Parameters of the Model

The inter-industry transaction matrix along with its row vectors of collection of net production taxes and value added and column vectors of components of final demand and value of production (henceforth referred to as the IO table for convenience) is the chief source of information for constructing the parameters of our 34-sector model. The other principal sources of data are the Annual Survey of Industries, and National Account Statistics (henceforth referred as ASI and NAS for convenience) of the Central Statistical Organisation of the Government of India. Information is also drawn from various other publications, and we shall refer to them as we discuss the methodology for constructing various parameters of the model. All of the pertinent data and parameters are to be found in appendix 2. Further information is available from the authors on request.

In the discussion below, variables and parameters are identified as listed in Appendix 1. Sets of sectors are indicated as in appendix tables A.1 and A.2.

Construction of IO Table

Our IO table is constructed from the 60-sector absorption and make matrices of the Planning Commission (Government of India), 1989–90. These are principally a price updated "Input-Output Transaction Table, 1983–84," of The Central Statistical Organisation (Government of India). We have used these matrices to compute the 60-sector commodity by commodity matrix under the commodity-technology assumption. This matrix is then aggregated into 34 sectors to arrive at a 34×34 flow matrix.[15] Understandably, aggregation poses a problem in some of the sectors because of the need to map the 60×60 matrix into two or more of our 34 sectors. Whenever this happened, we computed proportions based on the original 115×115 commodity-by-commodity matrix for the year 1983–84 and applied the same proportions to the 60×60 matrix to decompose such sectors. Apart from providing information on interindustry flows, our IO table provides sector-wise data on components of final demand (viz., private final consumption expenditure, government final consumption expenditure, gross fixed investment, changes in inventories, exports and imports) along the columns, and along the rows, sector-wise data on net indirect taxes less subsidies, gross value added and gross value of output. However, as the data for trade in services (i.e., ISIC sectors codes 5 to 9) in the IO table are deficient, we have adjusted the figures using information from the Michigan Model Database.

It should be noted that India's indirect taxes are distinguished as commodity taxes and other indirect taxes. The commodity taxes include: excise duties; sales taxes; custom duties (on exports and imports) and various other duties. The Other indirect taxes include levies such as those on electricity, motor vehicles, the entertainment tax and stamp duty, etc. For our study, as we will see later, we have decomposed indirect taxes less subsidies into three parts: export duties, import duties and other indirect taxes net of subsidies.

Demand Elasticity of India's Exports and Imports (η_j^R and η_j^M, $j \in TRS$)

The demand elasticity of India's exports appears directly as a parameter in the equation determining exports in our model whereas the demand elasticity of India's imports is required for deriving the elasticity of substitution between varieties of goods (σ_j), another parameter of the model.

The estimation of elasticities at our level of disaggregation is a time consuming and difficult task due to the limited availability of Indian data. For the present work, we have culled demand elasticities from various other studies done in the Indian context. This is the standard procedure adopted by most CGE modelers in spite of the drawbacks of using incorrect estimates.[16]

Understandably, in the existing literature, elasticities have not been estimated exactly at our level of disaggregation. Hence, judgment is needed in constructing elasticity estimates. This is true especially in ISIC sectors 2–9. For ISIC sectors 1A to 2, we found some literature estimates of elasticities that could be adapted for our use. As tables 6 and 7 of appendix 2 show, the export demand elasticities vary from -0.92 to -5.43 and the import demand elasticities vary from -0.11 to -3.61.

Elasticity of Substitution Between Capital and Labor $(\overline{\sigma}_j, j \in TAGS^c)$

For the present study, we need estimates of substitution elasticities between capital and labor for each of the 30 ISIC sectors, 310 to 9. Chadha et al. (1995) have estimated these elasticities using India state-level, cross-section data from ASI for the years 1988–89 and 1989–90. Since the ASI data are given according to the National Industrial Classification System (versions 1970 and 1987), we first concorded them to our ISIC sectors, following the concordance scheme noted in tables 2 and 3 of appendix 2. The estimates were then computed by pooled least square regression techniques[17].

Substitution Elasticities in Agriculture $(\overline{\sigma}_{j2}$ *and* $\overline{\sigma}_{j3}, j \in TAGS)$

The Michigan Model Database provides an estimate of the substitution elasticity between capital and labor for the combined agricultural sector. We have assumed that this estimate also holds for substitution between land and capital and the composite of land/capital and labor for each of the four agricultural sectors.

Elasticities of Substitution Between Varieties $(\sigma_j, j \in TRS)$

We have two sets of estimates of elasticities of substitution between varieties of goods. The first is based on the estimates obtained from the Michigan Model Database, and the second includes our own computed estimates. For the present work, we have mostly used our own estimates. However, in sectors where our own estimates seem unusually high, we have used the Michigan estimates.

We have estimated the elasticities using the formula, specified below:[18]

$$\sigma_j = \frac{1}{\theta_j^I}\left[\eta_j^M - \theta_j^M\left(v_{jo} + \sum_{k \in TRS} vd_{jk}\varepsilon_k b_{jk}\right)\right]$$

where

$$\varepsilon_k = \frac{\theta_j^L}{\theta_j^K}\frac{\overline{\sigma}_j}{b_{jo}}$$

and the other parameters on the right-hand side are listed in appendix 1.

Share/Stock of Land Allocated to Various Agricultural Sectors (h_j^F and $h_j^F F^o$, $j \in TAGS$)

Information on the utilization of land by the four agricultural sectors is from the "Fertilizer Statistics, 1993–94" of the Fertilizer Association of India. This source provides data on utilization of land by major crops of India. They are aggregated according to our sectors, and we then derive the figures for the fractions of land allocated to the four agricultural sectors. The shares of land utilized for the four sectors are computed using these fractions and the data on total land stock drawn from Economic Survey, 1991–92 of the Government of India.

Share/Stock of Capital Employed in Various Sectors (h_j^K and $h_j^K K^o$, $j \in ALS$)

The NAS provides data on capital stock by the following broad sectors: (1) agriculture, forestry and fishing; (2) mining and quarrying; (3) manufacturing; (4) electricity gas and water supply; (5) construction; (6) trade; (7) hotels and restaurants; (8) railways; (9) other transport, storage and communication; (10) finance, insurance, real estate and business services; (11) community, social and personal services. The ASI data, concorded to our ISIC sectors, provide information on the stock of capital employed in the registered manufacturing sectors (viz. sectors of ISIC codes 310 to 38A) of our model. We have used the above concorded ASI data to derive the sectoral shares of capital stock for the registered manufacturing sectors. Finally, these shares are applied to the NAS data for the overall capital stock in the manufacturing sector to compute the figures of capital employed in the individual manufacturing sectors.

For ISIC sectors 2 to 9, we have used the NAS data to estimate the stock of capital employed in these sectors. The same has been done for the four agricultural sectors (1A to 1D).[19]

Finally, the stock of capital at the sectoral level was divided by the overall stock to arrive at the estimate of share parameters in our model.

Share of Total Labor Force Employed in Various Sectors (h_j^L and $h_j^L L^o$, $j \in ALS$)

The "Technical note to The 8th Plan of India" of the Planning Commission (Government of India) provides data on employment at the end of the financial year 1987–88 for the following broad categories: (1) agriculture, forestry and fishing; (2) mining and quarrying; (3) manufacturing; (4) electricity, gas and water supply; (5) construction; (6) trade; (7) transport, storage and communication; and (8) services.[20] The above document also provides information on the growth rate of employment by these broad sectors for the period 1983–84 to 1987–88. Applying these sectoral growth rates, we obtained estimates of the labor force working in these broad sectors at the end of the financial year 1989–90.

The ASI data, concorded to our model sectors, provide information on the number of employees working in the registered manufacturing sectors (i.e., sectors 310 to 38A). We have used these concorded ASI data to derive the fraction of the labor force working in each of the registered manufacturing sectors. Finally, these shares were applied to our estimated figure of the overall labor force in the manufacturing sector to compute the number of workers in the base period in the individual manufacturing sectors.

The number of employees working in the railways was obtained from "Annual Report" of the Ministry of Railways. Subtracting it out from our estimate of the labor force in transport, storage and communication, we derived the number of employees working in our sector 7B. For ISIC 2 to 6, we used our computed estimates of the labor force to calculate the number of workers working in these sectors in the base period.

To estimate the number of laborers engaged in the four agricultural sectors, we used our estimates of the total labor force engaged in agriculture, the capital/labor ratio in overall agriculture, and our estimates of capital stocks in the agricultural sectors. A similar procedure was applied for the services sectors 8 and 9. Finally, the number of employees at the sectoral level was divided by the overall figure to arrive at the estimates of share parameters in our model.

Number of Firms $(n_j, j \in TICS \cup TSMS)$

The concorded ASI sectoral data provide information on the number of firms operating in our ISIC sectors 310 to 38A. According to our assumption, ISIC sectors 356, 371, 372, 374, and 7A, are under state monopolies. Thus, we assume that there is only one firm operating in these sectors. For the remaining sectors under imperfect competition, we take as a proxy for the number of firms operating in these sectors the number of firms operating in the registered manufacturing sectors at this level of disaggregation. The data, as mentioned earlier, are obtained from ASI.

Sector Specific Import Tariff Rates $(t_j, j \in TRS)$

Information on customs revenue collection for the years 1989–90 and 1990–91 at 4-digit product codes of the Indian Trade Classification (Harmonised Series)

System was drawn from the various issues of the Statistics of the Custom and Excise Revenue Collection of the Indian Union, published by the Directorate General of Commercial Intelligence and Statistics (DGCIS). The import figures for these two years at 6-digit product codes of Indian Trade Classification System (Harmonised Series) were also obtained on magnetic tapes from the DGCIS. Both of these were aggregated to concord to our sectors. Dividing the sectoral collection figures by the respective import values, we calculated sectoral import tariffs for these two years. The sector-wise simple average of these two years was taken as the estimate of import tariffs in our models. We used an average since we observed in the data some cases of excess/due collection on account of custom duties in a year being adjusted with the figures for the following year. It should be mentioned that DGCIS data provide information on custom collection and imports of sectors of ISIC codes 1A to 2. We have assumed that there are no import tariffs on the ISIC 4 to 9.

Sector Specific Export Tariff Rates $(t_j^x, j \in TRS)$

Information on total collection of export tariffs was drawn from the budget document of the Ministry of Finance (Government of India). The "Technical Note on The Seventh Five Year Plan" of the Planning Commission (Government of India) provides information, for the year 1989–90, on the structure of export tariffs for the 60 sectors of the Input-Output Table of the Planning Commission. Multiplying the structure by the total collection for export tariffs and concording to our sectoral scheme, we derived the data for sector-wise collection on account of export tariffs for the year 1989–90. The latter was divided by sector-wise export figures to estimate export tariff rates.

Sector Specific Other Net Production Tax Rates $(NT_j, j \in ALS)$

Our constructed IO table provided information on collection by sectors on all kinds of indirect taxes less subsidies. We deducted the amounts that were represented by export/import taxes. The other production tax rate net of subsidies was then calculated by dividing the residual amount at the sectoral level by the respective output data.

Share of Imports Subject to Quantitative Restriction $(\theta_j^{MQ}, j \in TRS)$

The Export-Import Policy Document (April 1987 to March 1990) of the Ministry of Commerce (Government of India), supplemented by the studies of Sharma and Pursell (1996) and Aksoy and Ettori (1992), were used to estimate the proportion of sectoral imports subject to some degree of quantitative restriction in the base year 1989–90.[21] However, a straightforward classification in many cases was not possible, so we relied on our judgment in many cases.

Share of Exports Subject to Quantitative Restriction ($\theta_j^{XQ}, j \in TRS$)

Following the procedure of computing θ_j^{MQ}, we estimated the parameter θ_j^{XQ}.

Perceived Elasticity of Demand by an Indian Firm in Industry j on its Sales in India ($\eta_j, j \in TMCS$)

It can be shown that η_j satisfies the following relation:[22]

$$\eta_j = -\sigma_j + (\sigma_j - 1)\frac{\theta_j^I}{n_j}$$

where,

σ_j = elasticity of substitution between varieties of j,

θ_j^I = share of home good share in total expenditure on j,

n_j = number of firms in industry j.

The η_j is estimated from the values of these parameters in the above relation.

Labor's Share of Expenditure on Primary Inputs in Sector j ($\theta_{j1}^L, j \in TAGS^c$)

We estimated the values of this parameter for ISIC sectors 310 to 38A from the concorded all-India ASI data for the year 1989–90, by taking the ratio of the total compensation to employees and the gross value added in the respective sectors.[23] As mentioned earlier, ASI data pertain only to the registered manufacturing sectors. However, we have assumed these same values also for the unregistered manufacturing sectors.

For the remaining sectors 2 to 9, we calculated the values from NAS data of total compensation to workers and gross value added in the base year. Of course, as our sectoral breakdown is slightly different from that of NAS, some judgement was required to calculate the estimates.

Capital's Share of Expenditure on Primary Inputs in Sector j ($\theta_{j1}^K, j \in TAGS^c$)

By definition, the shares of expenditure on labor and capital in primary inputs add up to one. Using this fact and the estimated values of the θ_{j1}^L, we estimated this parameter.

Land's Share of Expenditure on Second-Stage Aggregate of Primary Inputs in Sector j (θ^F_{j3}, $j \in$ TAGS)

This parameter along with the other share parameter described below, relating to the cost structure in the agricultural sectors, are computed from the data given in "Cost of Cultivation of Principal Crops in India," of the Ministry of Agriculture, Government of India. This document provides information on fixed cost, land cost, operational cost, labor cost and bullock and machinery cost of the principal crops of India. We have aggregated the cost structure of the principal crops according to our sectoral breakdown. The parameter is then computed by taking the ratio of the land cost to the sum of the bullock and machinery cost and the land cost.

Capital's Share of Expenditure on Second-Stage Aggregate of Primary Inputs in Sector j (θ^K_{j3}, $j \in$ TAGS)

By definition, the shares of expenditure on land and capital in the second-stage aggregate of primary inputs add up to one. Using this fact and the estimated values of the θ^K_{j3}, we estimated this parameter.

Labor's Share of Expenditure on First-Stage Aggregate of Primary Inputs in Sector j (θ^L_{j2}, $j \in$ TAGS)

To estimate this parameter, we have used the earlier specified concorded data for the cost structure of the principal crops in India. The parameter is computed by dividing the figures of labor cost of the respective sectors by the sum of the costs of labor, bullock and machinery, and land of each sector.

Share of Composite Land/Capital Expenditure on First-Stage Aggregate of Primary Inputs in Sector j (θ^{KF}_{j2}, $j \in$ TAGS)

The parameter is computed as one minus labor's share of expenditure on the first-stage aggregate of primary inputs.

Variable Input Share of Total Cost in Sector j (θ^{MC}_j, $j \in$ ALS)

By definition, for the sectors in which the market structure is perfectly competitive (i.e., 1A to 1D), θ^{MC}_j is assumed to be one. We have also assumed that it takes the value of one for the sectors under public sector monopolies (i.e., 5 to 9) in production.

For the remaining sectors in which the market structure is monopolistically competitive, the variable cost share is equal to the ratio of marginal cost and the average cost. That is,

$$\theta_j^{MC} = MC_j/ATC_j,$$

where

MC_j = marginal cost for a typical firm in industry j

ATC_j = average total cost for a typical firm in industry j.

Since profits are zero, average total cost is equal to price. Also, the ratio of marginal cost and price is determined by the markup pricing rule given below:

$$P_j = MC_j/(1 + 1/\eta_j),$$

where η_j is the perceived elasticity of demand for a typical firm in industry j. Substitution yields us:

$$\theta_j^{MC} = 1 + 1/\eta_j.$$

The above relation is used to estimate this parameter.

Fixed Input Share of Total Cost in Sector j (θ_j^{FC}, $j \in ALS$)

By definition, θ_j^{FC} is one minus the variable input share of total cost in industry j. Substituting our estimates of θ_j^{MC} in the above relation, we derived the values of this parameter.

Variable Capital's Share of Total Capital Employed in Industry j in India (θ_j^{VK}, $j \in TICS$)

The share of total capital that is variable is determined from the variable cost share, capital's primary input cost share, θ_{j1}^{K}, and the primary input share of total cost b_{j0}. Capital is assumed to be the fixed cost's share of the total capital cost. That is,

$$\theta_j^{VK} = \frac{K_j^v}{K_j^f + K_j^v}$$

$$= \frac{rK_j^v/TC_j}{(rK_j^f + rK_j^v/TC_j}$$

$$= \frac{\theta_j^{MC}}{\theta_{j1}^{K} b_{j0}}$$

where,

K_j^f and K_j^v are respectively the share of fixed and variable capital in a typical firm in industry j. Substituting the values in the above relation, we derived this parameter.[24]

4.3 Solution Procedure

Our model, as mentioned earlier, is specified as a system of simultaneous linear equations relating changes in all of the economic variables of our model. Given the values of the coefficients in each of the equations, the linearity of the system implies that it can be solved, in principle, by any of a variety of means.

We have operationalized the present model using release 5.1 of the General Equilibrium Modelling Package (Gempack) Software Suite, developed at the Impact Project, Monash University (Australia) under the direction of Ken Pearson.

4.4 Reporting of Results

The solution of the model in Gempack yields percentage changes in all of the endogenous variables. Because of the details involved, we refrain from presenting all the results. Typically, we select a set of important variables at the sectoral level (export and import demand, domestic demand, gross domestic product, production, number of firms (whenever applicable), demand for primary inputs) whose percentage changes are reported. For some of the above variables, we multiply, if it makes economic sense, the percentage changes by the data values in order to express the results in terms of absolute values. Of course, we also report percentage changes of other important variables of the economy, like exchange rate, economic welfare, and real rates of return to the factors of production.

CHAPTER 5

Policy Simulations and Results

The process of major economic reforms undertaken in the Indian economy has completed more than six years of implementation. The economy has entered into a new phase of development directed towards becoming globally competitive through opening it up to trade, foreign investment, and technology inflows. The unilateral reform measures in the trade and domestic policies of India along with reforms of the tax-regime represent a significant departure from the policy framework of the past four decades and are important to the future course of the Indian economy. These have already been discussed in chapter 2. In this chapter, we evaluate the comparative static effects of selected trade and domestic policy reforms on output, trade, factor prices, economic welfare and the intersectoral allocation of resources using our India CGE model that has been developed for this purpose. The model has been documented in chapter 3 and its implementation discussed in chapter 4.

5.1 Analytical Framework

The India CGE model that we have developed in this study is especially suited to analyze the impact of changes in tariffs and NTBs on the economy. We have analyzed such impacts through simulations using three different scenarios: (1) retaining the product market imperfections (state monopolies and administered prices) as these existed in 1989–90; (2) assuming that the economy was free from such distortions; and (3) assuming that the economy was free from such distortions and an attempt is also made to rationalize the indirect-tax regime. Keeping this in view, experiments have been performed with trade liberalization under the three different scenarios. In particular, we have analyzed the following reforms in trade policy:

(1) Import Reforms: these refer to reductions in tariffs and NTBs on imports; and

(2) Import and Export Reforms: these refer to the above mentioned import reforms plus reduction in NTBs on exports.

The first set of simulations refers to trade liberalization while retaining the product market imperfections. The state monopolies and the price administered sectors continue to operate in the same way. The domestic policy reforms are thus assumed to maintain status quo. We refer to this as the *administered ver-*

sion of the model. The results are based on the assumption that the domestic policy with respect to the product market imperfections is not reformed.

The second set of simulations refers to trade liberalization under the assumption that the domestic reforms have already taken place. We refer to this as the *market version* of the model. It is assumed that before we introduce trade reforms, as indicated above, the economy has already removed the product market imperfections. Thus all the sectors that were under state monopoly in 1989–90 are assumed to have been opened up to private competition such that petroleum products and iron and steel now operate under monopolistic competition while mining and quarrying, electricity, gas and water and rail transport now operate under perfect competition. Thus, the prices are no longer taken to be "administered" in these sectors. We also assume that the sectors that were under some kind of administered price regime in 1989–90 now determine their own prices. This amounts to doing away with administered prices in two agricultural sectors (paddy and wheat), and in three manufacturing sectors (paper products, fertilizer and non-ferrous metals). The paddy and wheat sectors are now assumed to determine their respective prices under perfect competition while the three manufacturing sectors determine their respective prices under monopolistic competition. Domestic capital is now mobile across all sectors.

The third set of simulations refers to trade liberalization under the *market version* of the model along with reducing subsidies (through increasing net indirect taxes) in the agricultural sectors, fertilizer, and electricity, gas and water supply, and reducing excise duties (through reducing net indirect taxes) on the remaining sectors of the Indian economy. These changes in indirect taxes are superimposed on the experiments with import and export liberalization under the domestically liberalized economy (market version) as discussed above in the second set of simulations.

5.2 Assumptions Regarding the Extent of the Trade Policy Reforms

The ongoing process of trade policy reforms is expected to result in reduction in tariffs on imports and NTBs to trade compared to what these were in 1989–90. The tariff on exports was nearly zero as of 1989–90. However, there were NTBs on export of some goods, mainly agricultural products. Though the process of major economic reforms commenced from 1991–92, we consider 1989–90 as the base year and assume that all the changes took place since that year. We make the following assumptions with regard to the reduction in import tariffs and NTBs to trade.

5.2.1 Import Reforms

These include reductions in tariffs and NTBs on imports. As per the Tariff Reforms Committee (Chelliah Committee) Interim Report (table 8.2 and para

TABLE 5.1. Proposed Tariff Rates

		Import Weighted Average		
	Import Weight	1989-90	1995-96	1998-99
Agricultural Products	0.03	46	20	15
Coal, crude oil, natural gas	0.16	54	34	25
Other mineral products	0.03	20	15	10
Manufactured Products	0.78	98	49	25
Consumer goods	0.07	89	60	50
Intermediate goods	0.47	103	45	30
Capital goods	0.24	91	55	30
Import Weighted Average	1.00	87	45	25

Source: Adapted from Tariff Reforms Committee (Chelliah Committee) Interim Report (table 8.2 and para 8.47) and Final Report-II (para 2.11).

8.47) and Final Report-II (para 2.11), the import weighted average declared duty is to be reduced from 87% in 1989–90 to 45% in 1995–96 and to 25% in 1998–99. The reduction to 25% may even be achieved by 1997–98. Details are given in table 5.1.

The collection rate was 50.4% in 1989–90. It has already come down to 29% in 1994–95. It may go down further to 25% by 1998–99. We will refer to the period 1989–90 to 1995–96 as *Stage I* and the longer period 1989–90 to 1998–99 as *Stage II*.

The NTBs (1989–90) on imports are assumed to be partially relaxed so as to permit a "fixed" percent increase in the imports that had been constrained. This is implemented in the model by increasing the level of imports that were under some kind of quantitative restriction for the sectors subject to import NTBs. Handling NTBs in such a manner is by no means satisfactory, but our rationale here is that the existing NTBs are not expected to be completely eliminated at the end of Stage II. We have attempted to analyze the effect of the two Scenarios of the relaxation of NTBs on imports noted in table 5.2.

These estimates in table 5.2 are not based on any actual declared numbers. However, we have tried to incorporate the implicit intentions in various policy announcements whereby the imports of agricultural and consumer goods are likely to remain more restricted than those of intermediate and capital goods as well as services. Thus, these estimates are indicative of the Indian Government's intentions towards the degree of expansion of imports that were under some type of quantitative restriction in 1989–90.

TABLE 5.2. Percent Increase (over 1989-90) in the Level of Imports under NTBs

	1989-90 to 1995-96	1989-90 to 1998-99
Agricultural Goods	10	25
Consumer Goods	25	50
Intermediate Goods	75	85
Capital Goods	75	85
Services	75	85

Source: Our estimates.

5.2.2 Export Reforms

These refer to reduction only in NTBs to exports, since tariff barriers on exports were negligible as of 1989–90. As with NTBs on imports, the existing NTBs (1989–90) on exports are assumed to be partially relaxed so as to permit a "fixed" percent increase in the exports that had been constrained. This is implemented in the model by increasing the level of exports that were under some kind of quantitative restriction for the sectors subject to export NTBs. Again, we have assumed here that the NTBs on exports are not expected to be completely removed as of Stage II. We have attempted to analyze the effect of the proposed relaxation of export NTBs noted in table 5.3. These estimates are based on the government's intention to open up exports of agricultural goods at a slower rate compared to other sectors.

TABLE 5.3. Percent Increase in Constrained Exports

	1989-90 to 1995-96	1989-90 to 1998-99
Agricultural Sectors	25	50
Other sectors	50	75

Source: Our estimates.

5.2.3 Rationalization of Indirect Taxes

We have already discussed in chapter 2 the indirect tax reforms suggested by the Tax Reforms Committee. In this study, we do not undertake a detailed analysis of the sectoral impact of changes in the excise-duty structure. Instead, we have performed a simple experiment on indirect tax rationalization which may be improved upon later. It is assumed that subsidies (net indirect taxes) are reduced in each of the four agricultural sectors, in the fertilizer sector and in electricity, gas and water supply. In all the remaining 28 sectors, the indirect taxes are assumed to be reduced through reduction of excise duties. The estimates are noted in table 5.4.

TABLE 5.4. Percent Reductions in Indirect Taxes and Subsidies

	1989-90 to 1995-96	1989-90 to 1998-99
Reduction of subsidies to four agricultural sectors, fertilizer, and electricity, gas and water supply	5	10
Reduction of indirect taxes in 28 other sectors	5	10

Source: Our estimates.

5.3 The Process of Gains

It is expected that trade liberalization will stimulate production of labor-intensive sectors in India. Productive resources will then be allocated more efficiently as compared to the pre-liberalization situation, as India specializes in the production of tradable goods in which it has comparative advantage. There may of course be transitional costs due to intersectoral movement of factors of production. Beyond such conventional welfare gains, trade liberalization is also expected to have a "pro-competitive" effect on domestic firms, resulting also in additional gains from the realization of economies of large scale production. When firms are protected by tariffs and NTBs from foreign competition, they may take advantage of their market power by raising their prices and reducing their domestic sales. The result is that the protected firms may produce at levels below their minimum-cost plant size. Trade liberalization should then bring about competitive pressures on formerly protected firms and induce them to raise production and productivity and to achieve more efficient plant size and lower per unit costs. Thus, the gains in economic welfare are expected to come from improved allocation of resources, lower prices to consumers and business firms, and availability of more varieties to consumers and firms. The realization of economies of scale in manufacturing also reinforces the welfare-enhancing effect.

The gains from the liberalization scenarios under study should, however, be treated as a lower bound. That is, we have abstracted from the effects of macroeconomic forces and policies and are not able to capture the effects of possible dynamic changes in efficiency and economic growth. We have also not analyzed the effects of potential inflows of foreign direct investment during the period under analysis. Thus, the gains we report are the result of reductions only in tariffs and NTBs on trade along with rationalization of the structure of net indirect taxes and subsidies. Further, we have also not been able to model the benefits to the Indian economy as a result of the unilateral reductions in trade barriers by the countries of ROW and the multilateral reductions to be implemented in meeting Uruguay Round obligations.[25]

The reduction in import tariffs and NTBs leads to a decline in the sectoral tariff equivalents (tariff plus tariff equivalent of import NTBs), which are endogenously determined in this model. The currency will depreciate in order to keep the base-year balance of trade at the same level. Consequently, the sectoral export tax equivalents (export tax plus export tax equivalent of export NTBs) will tend to increase. World prices are assumed to be exogenous. Therefore, the changes in import prices depend on two opposing forces: (1) the declining import tariff equivalents which tend to make imports cheaper; and (2) the depreciating currency which tends to make imports costlier. However, the currency depreciation gets an opposing push from the increased demand for Indian goods by ROW, many of which are now cheaper than before.

The changes in world prices of India's goods also depend on two opposing forces: (1) the increasing export tax equivalents which tend to make exports costlier; and (2) the depreciating currency which tends to make exports cheaper. Consequently, both import prices and domestic prices in most of the sectors decline, resulting in increases in exports as well as imports. If the export NTBs are also reduced, the export tax equivalent moves downward, thus giving a further push to sectoral exports.

The domestic price of a representative firm declines in almost all the cases except for the four agricultural sectors (sectors 1 to 4) and the two services sectors (sectors 34 and 35). These are the sectors that have a very high value added content. Since all the primary factors of production now have become costlier, the overall domestic price rises in these sectors. This increase in domestic prices of agricultural goods leads to improvement in the terms of trade between agriculture and manufacturing in favor of agriculture. The domestic prices of wood products and furniture and fixtures also increase since these depend on now costlier raw materials (wood) from agriculture.

5.4 Gains from Liberalization

As already noted, India has undertaken unilateral trade reforms since 1991–92. Under the import policy reforms, both tariffs and NTBs have been reduced. The economy has also further opened up on the export side by reducing export incentives as well as NTBs. The rupee exchange rate has been made flexible subject to market forces. The domestic policy reforms attempt to eliminate or reduce various product market imperfections, such as state monopolies, administered prices, etc. in certain sectors of the economy. Further, the structure of indirect taxes on production along with subsidies is undergoing major reforms.

The effects of these reforms have been calculated by our model for the various scenarios discussed earlier. Major results are shown in table 5.5 for the short-term effect that we label Stage 1 and that we associated with the period 1989-90 to 1995-96. Table 5.6 reports the same variables for the longer period, Stage II, from 1989-90 to 1998-99.

To understand these results, we recall from above that the economy's resources are re-allocated more efficiently as a result of the unilateral trade reforms. The resultant efficiency gains are higher if the product market imperfections in the economy are absent. GDP (a proxy for welfare) therefore increases and there may be gains in real returns to all three factors of production (land, labor and capital). In addition, because previous policies were largely protective of manufacturing at the expense of agriculture, the domestic terms of trade between the two sectors shifts in favor of agriculture.

Increase in GDP

It may be observed from tables 5.5 and 5.6 that the economy gains in real GDP (a proxy for welfare) when trade-policy reforms are undertaken. The increase in GDP is 1.1 percent with reduction in import restrictions and 1.3 percent with concurrent reduction in export restrictions (table 5.5) during Stage I under the *administered version* of the model. It rises to 3.1 percent in the *market version* of the model. The GDP growth increases to 3.2 percent when we allow for rationalization of the indirect tax regime under *market version*.

A similar picture emerges from the analysis of table 5.6 (Stage II). Thus, India's real GDP has the potential to be pushed up by about 5 percent as a result of sectoral re-adjustment that is expected to occur if we undertake the above mentioned trade and domestic policy reforms. The gains in GDP from the different experiments and model versions are depicted graphically in figure 5.1.

Figure 5.1. Overall Percentage Change in GDP from Unilateral Liberalization For Both Stage I and II of Administered and Market Versions of the Model

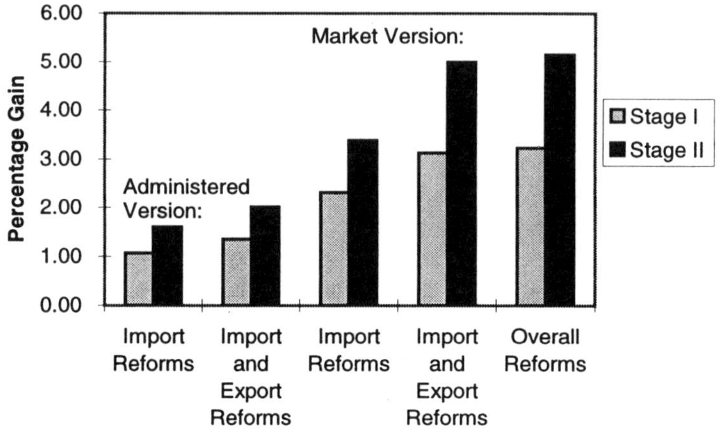

Overall Reforms represents trade reforms plus domestic policy reforms and rationalization of indirect taxes.

Gains in Returns to Factors of Production

An important gain to the economy comes from higher real returns to all three factors of production. It may be observed from tables 5.5 and 5.6 that all three factors (land, labor and capital) gain in real terms nearly by the same proportion as the increase in GDP. Thus, contrary to the Stolper-Samuelson Theorem, even the relatively scarce factors of production (land and capital) gain when tariffs against imports are lowered. The expected gains in factor returns increase from a range of 1.0 to 1.5 percent when the economy reduces import tariffs and NTBs under the administered version of the model to a range of 3.2 to 3.4 percent when the economy undertakes trade reforms (both import and export) under the market version. The factor returns rise a lot further if we allow for rationalization of the indirect tax regime under the market version. A similar picture emerges from the results in table 5.6 (Stage II). Thus, the real returns to the factors of production have the potential to increase by more than 4.5 percent as a result of the sectoral re-adjustment that is expected to occur if we undertake the above mentioned trade and domestic policy reforms. The gains in real returns to the factors of production are depicted graphically in figure 5.2.

Figure 5.2. Overall Changes in Returns to Factors of Production From Unilateral Liberalization, Stage II

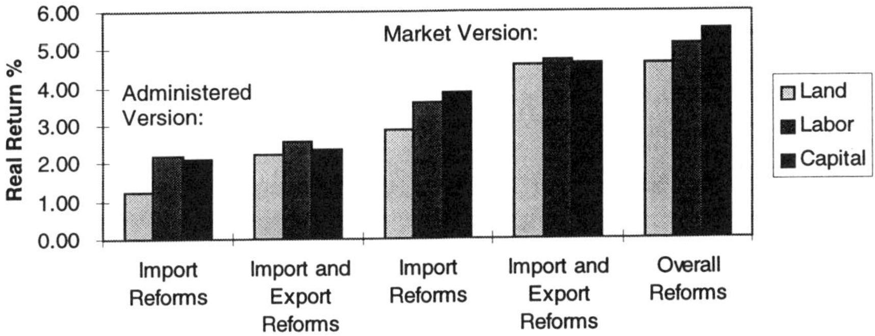

Terms of Trade Between Agriculture and Manufacturing

One of the important issues of the reform process in India is how the domestic terms of trade between agriculture and industry may be affected. The tariff reductions and deregulation in the industrial sector are expected to change the terms of trade between agriculture and industry in favor of agriculture (Gulati and Chadha, 1995). This is borne out in tables 5.5 and 5.6. The terms-of-trade shift in favor of agriculture increases from 2.2 percent when the economy undertakes import reforms under the administered version of the model to 6.1 percent when the economy undertakes imports and export reforms under the market version. The gains in terms of trade in favor of agriculture vis-a-vis manufacturing are depicted in figure 5.3.

Figure 5.3. Overall Changes in Domestic Terms of Trade (Agriculture vs Manufacturing, Percent)

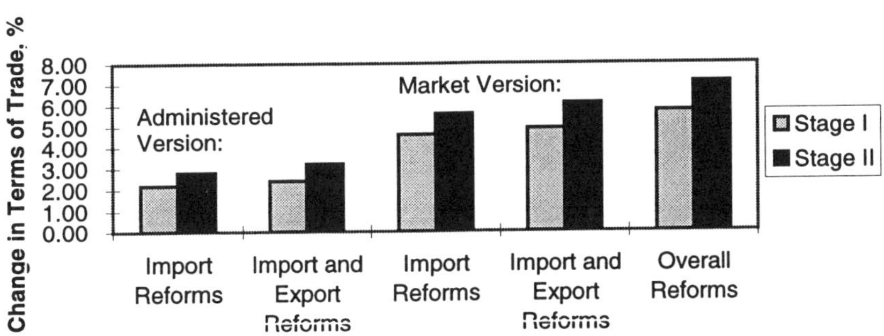

TABLE 5.5. Overall Changes from Unilateral Liberalization – Stage I (1989-90 to 1995-96)

	Trade Reforms (Administered Version)		Trade and Domestic Policy Reforms (Market Version)		Trade and Domestic Policy Reforms and Indirect Tax Rationalization
	Import Reforms	Import and Export Reforms	Import Reforms	Import and Export Reforms	Overall
Real GDP	1.07	1.35	2.32	3.13	3.23
Real Returns					
Land	1.00	1.55	2.32	3.19	3.23
Labor	1.62	1.88	2.80	3.40	3.63
Capital	1.471	1.66	2.87	3.34	3.77
Currency Depreciation	27.82	22.09	29.59	22.39	22.21
Terms of Trade (Agr vs Mfg)	2.20	2.40	4.60	5.74	

TABLE 5.6. Overall Changes from Unilateral Liberalization – Stage II (1989-90 to 1998-99)

	Trade Reforms (Administered Version)		Trade and Domestic Policy Reforms (Market Version)		Trade and Domestic Policy Reforms and Indirect Tax Rationalization
	Import Reforms	Import and Export Reforms	Import Reforms	Import and Export Reforms	Overall
Real GDP	1.60	2.01	3.38	5.00	5.15
Real Returns					
Land	1.26	2.24	2.89	4.57	4.64
Labor	2.19	2.58	3.62	4.70	5.16
Capital	2.11	2.36	3.85	4.64	5.53
Currency Depreciation	38.29	29.57	38.21	26.63	26.33
Terms of Trade (Agr vs Mfg)	2.80	3.20	5.60	6.10	7.10

5.5 Sectoral Results

5.5.1 Output, Number of Firms and Scale Effects

The changes in sectoral output, number of firms and scale effect (output per firm) are given in table 5.7. We have reported such changes only for Stage II. The largest increases in output occur in clothing, followed closely by leather products. The next highest output-increasing sectors are: footwear; glass products; and non-metallic mineral products. This is true of all the scenarios under the market version. The major sectors in which output declines include: nonferrous metals; nonelectrical machinery; and mining and quarrying; paper products; fertilizer; iron and steel; metal products; electrical machinery; transport equipment; and other transport, storage and communications. The output of cereals declines while that of the rest of agriculture increases. The overall agricultural output, however, registers a positive growth.

The change in the number of firms has only been analyzed for the 22 manufacturing sectors, which all are modeled (in the market version) as monopolistically competitive. The change in the direction of number of firms is consistent with the change in the direction of output of different sectors. The scale effect, which is the percent change in the output per firm, turns out to be positive in all the manufacturing sectors. The highest scale effect is observed in the footwear sector in which the output per firm gains by about 9 percent under the import and export reforms of Stage II. This is followed by petroleum products and glass products where the scale effect is close to 6 percent. A scale effect between 4 and 5 percent is observed in: clothing, leather products; fertilizer; and non-metallic mineral production. A scale effect between 2 and 3 percent is observed in: textiles; paper products; other chemicals; rubber products; and nonferrous metals. While the scale effect turns out to be substantial for a few sectors that are relatively labor intensive, the capital intensive sectors do not benefit equally. Iron and steel, nonelectrical machinery, electrical machinery and transport equipment experience only 1 percent increases in scale effects.

The relationship between the capital-labor ratio of 22 manufacturing sectors and changes in output and the scale effect (market version under Stage II) is shown in table 5.8 and figure 5.4. It may be observed from figure 5.4 that the sectors with low capital-labor ratios, i.e. the labor intensive sectors, experience higher percent gains in output as compared to the capital intensive sectors. This has important implications for employment in the country. Figure 5.5 depicts the relationship between the capital-labor ratio and change in output per

Figure 5.4. Capital-Labor Ratio vs % Change in Output

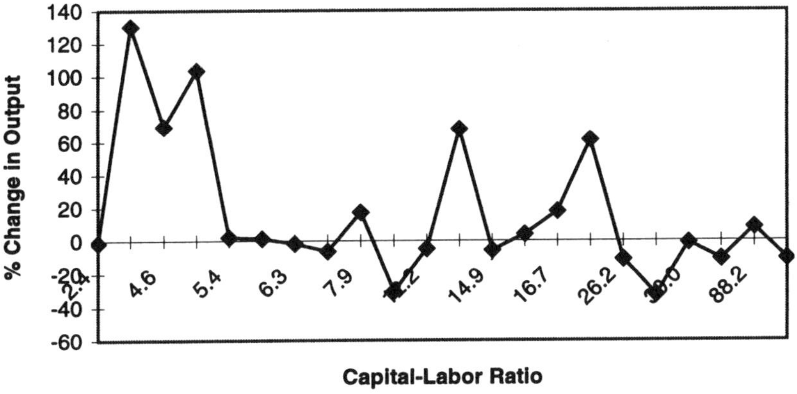

Figure 5.5. Capital-Labor Ratio vs % Scale Effect

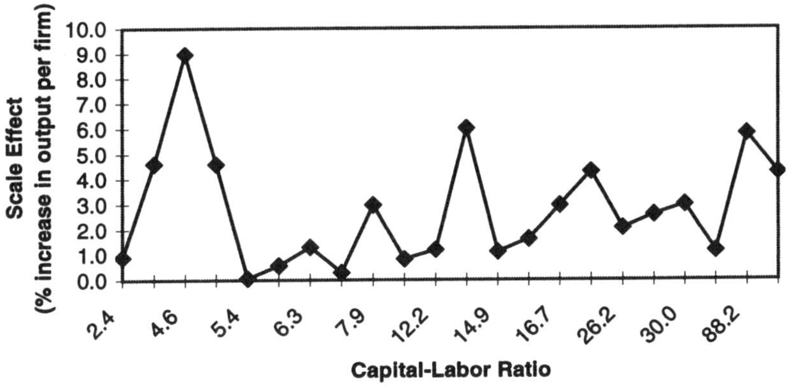

TABLE 5.7. Changes in Output, Number of Firms, and Scale Effects – Stage II

		Trade and Domestic Policy Reforms Market Version						Trade and Domestic Policy Reforms and Indirect Tax Rationalization		
		Import Reforms			Import & Export Reforms			Import & Export Reforms		
SN Sectors	ISIC	Output	No. of Firms	Scale Effect	Output	No. of Firms	Scale Effect	Output	No. of Firms	Scale Effect
1. Paddy	1A	-1.3			-1.1			-1.5		
2. Wheat	1B	-1.1			-1.4			-2.0		
3. Other Cereals	1C	-1.4			-1.7			-1.9		
4. Rest of Agriculture	1D	1.3			1.7			1.6		
5. Food, Bev. & Tobacco	310	1.5	0.9	0.6	1.5	0.9	0.6	1.5	0.3	1.2
6. Textiles	321	16.5	13.7	2.8	17.3	14.3	3.0	17.3	13.5	3.8
7. Clothing	322	122.6	118.2	4.4	130.4	125.8	4.6	127.2	122.1	5.1
8. Leather Products	323	93.6	89.4	4.2	103.5	98.9	4.6	102.3	97.0	5.3
9. Footwear	324	64.6	56.5	8.1	69.4	60.4	9.0	68.8	59.1	9.7
10. Wood Products	331	2.2	2.1	0.2	2.2	2.1	0.1	2.8	2.3	0.5
11. Furniture Fixtures	332	-0.8	-1.7	0.9	-1.1	-2.0	0.9	-0.9	-2.4	1.5
12. Paper Products	341	-10.7	-12.6	1.9	-11.2	-13.3	2.1	-10.6	-13.8	3.2
13. Printing & Publishing	342	-1.3	-2.5	1.2	-1.6	-2.9	1.3	-1.2	-3.7	2.4
14. Fertilizer	35A	-10.7	-14.5	3.9	-10.8	-15.0	4.3	-11.0	-16.2	5.1
15. Other chemicals	35B	-0.8	-3.5	2.7	-1.0	-3.9	3.0	0.0	-4.7	4.8
16. Petroleum Products	35C	6.8	1.3	5.5	8.3	2.5	5.8	9.9	0.7	9.3
17. Rubber Products	355	16.3	13.5	2.7	17.9	15.0	3.0	19.0	14.3	4.7
18. Non-metallic Min. Prod.	36A	54.3	50.2	4.0	61.2	56.9	4.3	61.2	55.9	5.3
19. Glass Products	362	60.0	54.5	5.4	67.9	61.9	6.0	68.6	61.1	7.5
20. Iron & Steel	371	-8.3	-9.5	1.3	-11.0	-12.1	1.2	-9.2	-12.3	3.1
21. Non-ferrous Metal	372	-27.2	-29.7	2.5	-32.5	-35.1	2.6	-29.2	-33.8	4.6
22. Metal Products	381	-4.5	-4.9	0.4	-6.4	-6.7	0.3	-5.0	-7.0	2.0

		Trade and Domestic Policy Reforms Market Version						Trade and Domestic Policy Reforms and Indirect Tax Rationalization		
		Import Reforms			Import & Export Reforms			Import & Export Reforms		
SN Sectors	ISIC	Output	No. of Firms	Scale Effect	Output	No. of Firms	Scale Effect	Output	No. of Firms	Scale Effect
23. Non-electrical Machinery	382	-25.4	-26.2	0.9	-30.6	-32.4	0.8	-27.6	-30.2	2.6
24. Electrical Machinery	383	-4.8	-5.9	1.1	-5.8	-6.9	1.1	-3.9	-7.1	3.2
25. Transport Equipment	384	-4.3	-5.5	1.2	-4.7	-5.9	1.2	-3.3	-6.3	3.0
26. Misc. Manufacturing	38A	3.8	2.3	1.6	3.9	2.2	1.6	5.2	1.5	3.8
27. Mining & Quarrying	2	-27.5			-25.9			-24.5		
28. Electricity, Gas & Water	4	2.3			2.3			2.7		
29. Construction	5	0.8			0.7			1.4		
30. Wholesale & Retail Trade	6	2.6			2.4			2.5		
31. Rail Transport	7A	0.5			0.4			1.1		
32. Other Transport, Storage & Com	7B	-2.7			-3.2			-2.5		
33. Finance, Ins. & Real Est.	8	-0.7			-0.9			-0.9		
34. Comm., Social & Pers. Serv.	9	-0.2			-0.4			-0.2		

firm (scale effect). It may be observed that the scale effect is higher for more capital intensive sectors than in less capital intensive sectors. Thus the scarce factor of production (capital) is expected to become more effectively utilized.

5.5.2 Intersectoral Movement of Labor and Capital

As is evident in table 5.9, labor and capital move into the sectors that now produce more and vice versa. Thus, labor and capital move towards sectors such as: clothing; leather products; footwear; glass products; and non-metallic mineral products; and away from: nonferrous metals; nonelectrical machinery; mining and quarrying; paper products; fertilizer; and iron and steel. In agriculture, land, labor and capital move out of cereals to other agriculture.

5.5.3 Exports and Imports

Exports

The details of gains in exports and imports in the 33 traded sectors of the Indian economy are provided in table 5.10. The sectors with the largest export increases include: textiles; clothing; footwear; iron and steel; electrical machinery; transport equipment; and misc. manufacturing. Exports also increase notably in: food; beverages and tobacco; leather products; furniture; paper products; printing and publishing; fertilizer; petroleum products; rubber products; nonmetallic mineral products; glass products; nonferrous metals and mineral products; printing and publishing; fertilizer; petroleum products; rubber products; nonmetallic mineral products; glass products; nonferrous metals and mining and quarrying. However, if domestic policy reforms are also undertaken along with trade policy reforms, some of the very high export gaining sectors lose their position, with some other sectors higher than before, including: clothing and footwear; textiles; leather products; nonmetallic mineral products; and glass products.

It may also be noted that the exports of the agricultural sectors, fertilizer, petroleum products, and mining and quarrying show impressive gains in export growth when export NTBs are also reduced along with import liberalization. This is true under the administered as well as the market version of the model.

TABLE 5.8. Capital Labor Ratio vs. Output Gain and Scale Effect

Manufacturing Sectors	ISIC	K/L Ratio	Output Gain	Scale Effect
Furniture Fixtures	332	2.4	-1.1	0.9
Clothing	322	3.2	130.4	4.6
Footwear	324	4.6	69.4	9.0
Leather Products	323	5.0	103.5	4.6
Wood Products	331	5.4	2.2	0.1
Food, Bev. & Tobacco	310	5.9	1.5	0.6
Printing & Publishing	342	6.3	-1.6	1.3
Metal Products	381	7.4	-6.4	0.3
Textiles	321	7.9	17.3	3.0
Non-Electrical Machinery	382	11.8	-30.6	0.8
Transport Equipment	384	12.2	-4.7	1.2
Glass Products	362	12.5	67.9	6.0
Electrical Machinery	383	14.9	-5.8	1.1
Misc. Manufacturing	38a	15.1	3.9	1.6
Rubber Products	355	16.7	17.9	3.0
Non-Metallic Min. Prod.	36a	22.4	61.2	4.3
Paper Products	341	26.2	-11.2	2.1
Non-Ferrous Metal	372	28.2	-32.5	2.6
Other Chemicals	35b	30.0	-1.0	3.0
Iron & Steel	371	43.9	-11.0	1.2
Petroleum Products	35c	88.2	8.3	5.8
Fertilizer	35a	100.0	-10.8	4.3

TABLE 5.9. Intersectoral Movement of Factors of Production – Stage II (Percent)

SN Sectors	ISIC	Trade Reforms Administered Version				Trade and Domestic Policy Reforms Market Version				Trade and Domestic Policy Reforms and Indirect Tax Rationalization	
		Import Reforms		Import & Export Reforms		Import Reforms		Import & Export Reforms		Overall	
		Labor	Capital	Labor	Capital	Labor	Capital	Labor	Capital	Labor	Capital
1. Paddy	1A	-0.6	-0.5	-0.3	0.1	-1.3	-0.6	-1.0	-0.2	-1.5	-0.9
2. Wheat	1B	-0.7	-0.6	-0.8	-0.5	-1.2	-0.5	-1.4	-0.6	-2.0	-1.5
3. Other Cereals	1C	-1.1	-1.1	-1.2	-1.2	-1.5	-0.8	-1.7	-0.9	-1.9	-1.4
4. Rest of Agriculture	1D	-1.1	0.9	1.5	1.6	1.3	2.0	1.8	2.6	1.6	2.2
5. Food, Bev. & Tobacco	310	1.3	1.2	1.3	1.3	1.0	1.6	1.0	1.6	1.0	1.4
6. Textiles	321	9.8	9.7	10.1	10.1	15.7	16.4	16.5	17.3	16.4	17.0
7. Clothing	322	48.6	43.5	51.1	51.2	119.,6	120.7	127.1	128.4	124.1	124.9
8. Leather Products	323	56.7	55.6	62.3	62.4	92.4	93.3	102.1	103.3	101.0	101.8
9. Footwear	324	35.9	35.9	38.2	38.2	63.2	63.7	67.8	68.3	67.2	67.6
10. Wood Products	331	1.0	1.0	0.9	1.0	1.9	2.5	1.8	2.5	2.5	3.0
11. Furniture Fixtures	332	-0.9	-1.0	-1.2	-1.2	-1.4	-0.4	-1.7	-0.6	-1.7	-0.9
12. Paper Products	341	0.8	0.7	0.5	0.6	-11.6	-10.7	-12.3	-11.2	-11.6	-10.8
13. Printing & Publishing	342	-1.6	-1.7	-2.0	-1.9	-2.2	-1.3	-2.6	-1.6	-2.6	-1.9
14. Fertilizer	35A	0.1	0.0	0.2	0.3	-11.7	-11.1	-12.0	-11.2	-12.2	-11.7
15. Other chemicals	35B	-2.7	-2.8	-3.2	-3.2	-1.6	-1.0	-2.0	-1.2	-1.1	-0.6
16. Petroleum Products	35C	4.6	0.0	22.8	0.0	4.5	6.2	5.7	7.6	7.4	8.7

SN Sectors	ISIC	Trade Reforms Administered Version: Import Reforms		Trade Reforms Administered Version: Import & Export Reforms		Trade and Domestic Policy Reforms Market Version: Import Reforms		Trade and Domestic Policy Reforms Market Version: Import & Export Reforms		Trade and Domestic Policy Reforms and Indirect Tax Rationalization: Overall	
		Labor	Capital	Labor	Capital	Labor	Capital	Labor	Capital	Labor	Capital
17. Rubber Products	355	11.8	11.7	12.8	12.9	15.2	16.2	16.7	17.9	17.8	18.6
18. Non-metallic Min. Prod.	36A	29.8	29.7	33.4	33.4	53.0	53.9	59.8	60.9	59.9	60.7
19. Glass Products	362	32.2	32.1	36.1	36.1	58.1	59.0	65.8	66.8	66.3	67.0
20. Iron & Steel	371	-36.6	0.0	-49.0	0.0	-9.0	-8.4	-11.8	-11.1	-10.1	-9.7
21. Non-ferrous Metal	372	-2.2	-2.3	-2.1	-2.1	-28.2	-27.3	-33.6	-32.6	-30.3	-29.7
22. Metal Products	381	-4.6	-4.7	-6.3	-6.2	-5.2	-4.3	-7.1	-6.0	-6.0	-5.3
23. Non-electrical Machinery	382	-22.7	-22.8	-28.1	-28.0	-26.1	-25.3	-31.4	-30.4	-28.8	-28.2
24. Electrical Machinery	383	-5.3	-5.4	-6.4	-6.3	-5.4	-4.7	-6.5	-5.7	-4.7	-4.2
25. Transport Equipment	384	-4.4	-4.4	-4.7	-4.7	-4.6	-4.2	-5.1	-4.5	-3.9	-3.5
26. Misc. Manufacturing	38A	1.7	1.6	1.5	1.5	3.1	3.8	3.1	3.9	4.3	4.8
27. Mining & Quarrying	2	7.5	0.0	15.1	0.0	-28.3	-26.9	-26.8	-25.2	-25.2	-24.1
28. Electricity, Gas & Water	4	4.8	0.0	5.0	0.0	1.1	3.2	1.0	3.4	1.8	3.4
29. Construction	5	0.1	0.0	-0.1	0.0	0.6	1.6	0.4	1.5	1.2	2.0
30. Wholesale & Retail Trade	6	1.5	1.4	1.1	1.3	1.4	3.5	1.1	3.5	1.6	3.2
31. Rail Transport	7A	0.3	0.0	0.2	0.0	0.4	1.7	0.3	1.9	1.1	2.1
32. Other Transport, Storage & Com	7B	-3.6	-3.7	-4.3	-4.2	-3.4	-2.1	-4.1	-2.6	-3.1	-2.1
33. Finance, Ins. & Real Est.	8	-0.6	-0.8	-1.0	-0.8	-1.6	-0.1	-1.9	-0.2	-1.6	-0.5
34. Comm., Social & Pers. Serv.	9	-0.3	-0.4	-0.5	-0.4	-0.3	0.7	-0.5	0.7	-0.2	0.5

Imports

When the economy undertakes reforms in trade policy alone (administered version), the growth of sectoral imports is substantial in: electrical machinery; transport equipment; wholesale and retail trade; other transport, storage and communications; and finance, insurance and real estate. The sectors with declines in import growth include clothing and commercial, social and personal services. The sectors that experience moderate decline in imports include wood products, iron and steel, and non-ferrous metals. The imports of rice and wheat show a very small decline.

If the economy also undertakes domestic policy reforms along with trade policy reforms (market version), the high import gaining sectors under the administered version remain so under the market version of the model. However, some of the sectors that experienced very small or even negative import growth under the administered version become high import growth sectors under the market version.

5.6 Sensitivity Analysis

The results of the model have been tested for their stability by analyzing their sensitivity to changes in some of the major parameters used in the model. We have done this exercise for five such parameters:

29. demand elasticity of India's exports to ROW;
2) elasticity of substitution among imported and domestic varieties of a good produced by representative firms/industry in India;
3) elasticity of substitution between capital and labor in the nonagricultural sectors in India;
4) elasticity of substitution between land and capital in India's agricultural sectors; and
5) elasticity of substitution between labor and the composite of land and capital in India's agricultural sectors.

The details on the roles of these parameters in the model as well as the values used for them in the model are given in preceding chapters.

A 10 percent increase in export demand elasticity values for each of the tradable sectors leads to less than 5 percent changes in GDP, total imports, total exports, real returns to the three factors of production, and the exchange rate depreciation. The major variables change by less than 4 percent when the values of the elasticity of substitution between imported and domestic varieties are increased by 10 percent each.

TABLE 5.10. Changes in Exports and Imports – Stage II (Percent)

SN Sectors	ISIC	Trade Reforms Administered Version: Import Reforms		Trade Reforms Administered Version: Import & Export Reforms		Trade and Domestic Policy Reforms Market Version: Import Reforms		Trade and Domestic Policy Reforms Market Version: Import & Export Reforms		Trade and Domestic Policy Reforms and Indirect Tax Rationalization: Overall	
		Exports	Imports	Exports	Imports	Exports	Imports	Exports	Imports	Exports	Imports
1. Paddy	1A	12.9	-0.9	51.1	-1.0	12.4	5.2	50.8	7.1	50.3	7.6
2. Wheat	1B	12.9	-0.8	51.1	-1.0	12.5	5.2	50.9	7.1	50.2	7.7
3. Other Cereals	1C	12.6	5.7	50.9	7.8	12.4	6.0	50.8	7.9	50.3	8.3
4. Rest of Agriculture	1D	25.3	-0.1	51.7	5.1	24.8	0.9	51.4	5.8	50.6	6.9
5. Food, Bev. & Tobacco	310	64.7	32.1	71.0	34.1	65.5	32.2	72.5	34.0	71.0	34.4
6. Textiles	321	83.6	9.0	88.2	15.0	97.0	8.1	103.1	13.6	102.0	14.2
7. Clothing	322	85.5	-24.8	90.3	-20.7	210.1	-51.2	223.8	-49.3	218.4	-47.1
8. Leather Products	323	67.4	22.0	74.7	24.7	108.4	20.1	120.7	22.2	119.2	22.7
9. Footwear	324	94.5	25.3	100.6	26.8	165.9	20.9	177.9	21.8	176.0	22.2
10. Wood Products	331	37.8	-12.2	70.1	-4.7	37.6	-11.2	70.3	-4.1	69.6	-2.8
11. Furniture Fixtures	332	61.2	39.71	68.0	43.0	59.8	40.1	66.9	43.2	66.1	43.6
12. Paper Products	341	61.1	0.5	68.0	0.4	62.0	53.2	69.6	55.5	69.5	55.6
13. Printing & Publishing	342	61.3	21.5	68.2	24.8	60.9	21.5	68.3	24.5	68.6	24.5
14. Fertilizer	35A	10.0	0.0	68.6	0.3	10.6	52.7	69.5	54.4	69.3	54.7
15. Other chemicals	35B	41.1	38.8	51.1	45.4	44.6	37.0	55.4	43.0	56.1	42.6
16. Petroleum Products	35C	10.0	0.2	68.6	0.3	11.7	-47.3	70.8	-38.0	71.5	-44.4
17. Rubber Products	355	62.6	35.3	70.2	42.5	73.9	33.4	83.2	39.8	84.5	39.3
18. Non-metallic Min. Prod.	36A	59.0	18.6	66.5	23.2	206.5	-2.3	120.3.	-0.8	119.6	0.5
19. Glass Products	362	61.9	1.7	69.9	6.0	111.5	-17.5	126.6	-16.3	127.1	-16.2
20. Iron & Steel	371	79.9	-4.0	84.2	-5.1	76.8	23.1	80.4	30.0	82.5	29.6

(continued)

Table 5.10. *(Continued)*

SN Sectors	ISIC	Trade Reforms Administered Version: Import Reforms		Import & Export Reforms		Trade and Domestic Policy Reforms Market Version: Import Reforms		Import & Export Reforms		Trade and Domestic Policy Reforms and Indirect Tax Rationalization: Overall	
21. Non-ferrous Metal	372	40.0	-3.3	79.6	-4.1	40.1	42.8	80.2	52.1	81.7	50.2
22. Metal Products	381	39.7	24.6	49.5	31.8	39.2	25.2	48.9	32.3	49.7	31.9
23. Non-electrical Machinery	382	55.6	35.1	63.5	42.5	57.2	35.8	65.7	42.9	67.1	41.9
24. Electrical Machinery	383	78.3	48.0	83.3	52.7	82.1	48.2	87.6	52.6	90.2	52.0
25. Transport Equipment	384	81.3	55.6	85.9	57.9	82.9	55.8	87.8	58.1	90.0	57.8
26. Misc. Manufacturing	38A	81.8	26.8	86.5	28.7	88.1	26.7	93.7	28.5	96.2	28.3
27. Mining & Quarrying	2	12.9	2.7	71.1	3.6	16.7	53.3	75.3	56.0	75.1	56.7
28. Electricity, Gas & Water	4	a4.0	2.2	12.1	2.3	14.6	42.4	12.9	455.4	12.4	46.3
29. Construction	5	28.8	42.2	25.2	45.4	29.6	41.7	26.3	44.6	26.6	44.5
30. Wholesale & Retail Trade	6	13.9	52.7	12.1	54.7	13.9	53.1	12.2	55.0	11.8	55.5
31. Rail Transport	7A										
32. Other Transport, Storage & Com	7B	14.0	48.5	12.2	50.8	15.2	48.5	13.6	50.6	13.8	50.5
33. Finance, Ins. & Real Est.	8	13.8	53.0	12.0	55.0	13.7	53.2	12.0	55.0	11.5	55.5
34. Comm., Social & Pers. Serv.	9	14.0	-25.1	12.2	-21.8	13.8	-24.8	12.1	-21.7	11.8	-21.2

The model results remain even more stable with 10 percent increases in the elasticities of substitution between the primary factors of production. There is nearly no change in any of the major variables when the elasticity of substitution between capital and labor in the nonagricultural sectors is increased by 10 percent. However, there is a minor change (0.2 percent) in the real return to land when each of the two measures of the elasticity of substitution between factors in India's agricultural sectors is increased by 10 percent.

It thus appears that the model results are not particularly sensitive to the values of the major parameters used in this study.

CHAPTER 6

Conclusions and Implications for Policy and Further Research

In this chapter, we summarize briefly the conclusions and implications of our study and indicate what we hope to accomplish in further research.

6.1 Conclusions and Implications for Policy

The Indian Government has introduced significant unilateral trade reforms since 1991–92. Under the import-policy reforms, both tariffs and NTBs have been reduced. The economy has been further opened up on the export side by reducing export incentives as well as barriers. The Indian rupee has been made flexible subject to market forces. Furthermore, the domestic policy reforms have sought to eliminate or reduce various product market imperfections, such as state monopolies and administered prices in certain sectors of the economy. Finally, the structure of indirect taxes on production along with subsidies has been undergoing major reform.

In an effort to determine the economic effects of these various policy changes, we have constructed a multisectoral CGE model of the Indian economy. Our computational results suggest percentage increases in India's GDP of up to 5 percent, depending on full implementation of the reforms. We also show increased real returns to land, labor, and capital, which are the three factors of production included in the model. The policy reforms appear to shift the terms of trade in favor of Indian agriculture. Lastly, not only are there efficiency enhancing intersectoral shifts in resource allocation, but there are notable scale economy increases across the Indian manufacturing sectors.

Our results reflect of course the particular assumptions that have been incorporated into our CGE modeling framework as well as the choice of parameters used. Granting this, we hope that our results will provide the basis for further analysis of the economic consequences of India's policy reforms and serve to support the future continuance of these reforms in an effort to enhance the nation's economic efficiency and welfare.

6.2 Agenda for Further Research

The CGE model and data base that we have developed in this study are but a first step in our research agenda. Some of the research that we plan for the future is as follows.

6.2.1. Link the India and Michigan CGE Models

As mentioned in our earlier discussion, the India CGE model is a stand-alone model based on the structure of the Michigan CGE multi-country model. Thus, in modeling the import and export sectors in the India model, we have included the rest-of-world (ROW) as an aggregate. What we plan to do next then is explicitly to link the India and Michigan models so that we can place the Indian economy in a global modeling framework. This will require developing a procedure to take into account the differences in sectoral coverage in the India and Michigan models. Once this is accomplished, it will then be possible to investigate the global effects of the Indian unilateral policy reforms that we have abstracted from in the present study. In addition, we will be able to analyze the economic effects of the Uruguay Round multilateral negotiations and future multilateral liberalization initiatives on India and its major trading partners. The Uruguay Round negotiations include reductions in multilateral tariffs and NTBs, phased elimination of the Multifibre Arrangement that will increase export opportunities in clothing and textiles for India and other developing countries, and phased reduction of agricultural protection especially in the major industrialized countries. In the coming years under the auspices of the newly created World Trade Organization (WTO), there will be liberalization of trade barriers in such service sectors as telecommunications and financial services. By linking the India and Michigan CGE models, it will therefore be possible to provide a much richer and more comprehensive analysis of the effects, both within India and in the global context, of the various policy changes already implemented as well as those that may be introduced in the future.

The linking of the India and Michigan models will also permit analysis of possible future regional trading arrangements in which India may be involved. As reported in Chadha et al. (1996), work has been initiated at NCAER to construct a data base for several of the most important trading nations in Asia, some of which are not represented explicitly at present in the Michigan model. The plan is to develop an Asian CGE submodel that can be used to analyze potential regional arrangements and to embed this submodel into the Michigan global framework so that the multilateral implications of the regional arrangements can be assessed in a broader context. The benefits and costs of Asian regional trade arrangements can in this way be measured and compared to those that would be realized if multilateral liberalization is pursued as an option.

6.2.2 Further Disaggregation of the India CGE Model

The present structure of the India CGE model is economy-wide. It therefore does not provide information on how India's policy reforms affect sectors at the state/regional levels and different occupational groups. It would be quite difficult to attempt to construct CGE models for individual states within India, especially since data on interstate trade is not available. But using available sectoral and occupational data broken down by state, we hope to be able to develop a method for breaking down the economy-wide results. This was done by, Brown, Deardorff, and Stern (1992) in their study of how the North American Free Trade Agreement (NAFTA) would affect sectors/occupational groupings at the state and regional levels in the United States. Something similar could be done for India. Although inevitably crude, it would nonetheless be informative to know how the policy reforms may have impacted the Indian economy on a more disaggregated geographic and occupational level.

6.2.3 Dynamic Growth Effects

Both the India and Michigan CGE models rely on a comparative static framework and therefore do not take dynamic growth effects into account. Examples of how CGE models can be adapted for this purpose are provided in some of the CGE studies of the results of the Uruguay Round reported in Martin and Winters (1996). While these adaptations tend to be ad hoc in character, they may nonetheless be indicative of how the policy reforms may affect capital accumulation especially and what the consequent growth impacts may be.

It would also be possible to develop a CGE model for India that uses a dynamic optimization framework in which the microeconomic and macroeconomic consequences of policy reforms are permitted to interact in the course of time. Models of this kind have been developed and implemented, for example, by Keuschnigg and Kohler (1996). Their advantage is that they provide an integrative modeling framework that may provide more insight than the more simple comparative static CGE models that have been so widely used to date.

Notes

Chapter 1

[1] For additional details, see Bhagwati and Srinivasan (1993) and Joshi and Little (1994).

[2] Details on India's post-1991 economic performance are to be found in Economic Survey (1996-97). See also Joshi and Little (1994).

Chapter 2

[3] The high growth rates achieved during the 1980s were based on excessive internal spending and both internal and external borrowing, and hence were clearly unsustainable. This in fact led directly to the huge crisis that forced the reforms in early 1990s.

[4] Some of the discussion in this section is based on Joshi and Little (1994, Ch. 2).

Chapter 3

[5] Marwah (1991) notes that 40 out of the 80 models developed for the Indian economy during the preceding four decades have been econometric models.

[6] Typically, the I-O tables in India are available with a lag of about 10 years.

[7] Resource allocation and investment planning are the key focus of planning models.

[8] An attempt in modelling the money market in India was also made in Mammen (1967).

[9] The latter is part of the LINK project.

[10] They include agriculture, manufacturing, infrastructure, services, public administration and defense.

[11] The disaggregated structure of the model with some dynamic elements built into it (through lagged structure and capital stock updating through investment) allows for detailed forecasts.

[12] In this aspect, this model follows their earlier model, namely Narayana et al. (1987).

[13] Restrictions on imports and exports have been modeled using estimates of net protection coefficients (NPC) from other studies which are in some cases ad hoc.

[14] For a detailed discussion of the use of CGE models for development policy analysis in less developed countries, see Bandara (1991).

Chapter 4

[15] See table 1 of appendix 2 below for details.

[16] In the future, we plan to estimate these demand elasticities ourselves.

[17] See Chadha, Pohit and Bina (1995) for details.

[18] The interested reader may consult Deardorff and Stern (1986, pp. 235-247) for the derivation.

[19] We have used the sector-wise output figure from our IO table and data for the capital/output ratio in agriculture, computed from NAS, to estimate the capital stock in the four agricultural sectors.

[20] The employment estimates are based on *Usual Principal Status.*

[21] Obviously, the so-called canalized commodities are subject to quantitative restriction.

[22] See Chadha, Djankov and Pohit (1995) for derivation.

[23] We have estimated total compensation by adding the other benefits, etc. to the total emoluments figures.

[24] However in some sectors, this leads to estimates greater than one. We have modified the estimates in these cases to reduce them to below one.

Chapter 5

[25] Because our CGE model is economy-wide and we distinguish only three factors of production, we cannot with our existing model structure determine how liberalization may affect states and regions within India and different types of workers.

References

Ahluwalia, I. J. 1979. *Behaviour of Prices and Outputs in India–A Macro-econometric Approach*, Macmillan, New Delhi.

Ahluwalia, Isher Judge. 1985. *Industrial Growth in India: Stagnation since the Mid-Sixties*, Oxford University Press, Delhi.

Ahluwalia, Isher Judge. 1993. "Industrial Policy Reform of Public Sector Enterprises and Privatisation in India," Paper presented at the *Conference on India—The Future of the Reforms*, held at Merton College, Oxford, June 1993.

Aksoy, A. and F. M. Ettori. 1992. "Protection and Industrial Structure in India," *Working Paper No. WPS 990*, Country Department, World Bank.

Alexander, P. C. (Chairman). 1977. "Report on the Committee on Import–Export Policies and Procedures," Ministry of Commerce, Government of India.

Bandara, Jayatilleke S. 1991. "Computable General Equilibrium Models for Development Policy Analysis in LDCs," *Journal of Economic Surveys*, 5(1), pp. 3–67.

Bhagwati, J. 1993. *India in Transition: Freeing the Economy*, Clarendon Press, Oxford.

Bhagwati, J. 1997. *Writings on International Economics.* New Delhi: Oxford University Press.

Bhagwati, Jagdish and T. N. Srinivasan. 1975. *Foreign Trade Regimes and Economic Development: India,* Columbia University Press, New York.

Bhagwati, Jagdish and T. N. Srinivasan. 1993. "India's Economic Reforms," Paper prepared for the Ministry of Finance, Government of India.

Bhattacharya, B. B., Barman, and A. K. Nag. 1994. "Stabilisation Policy Options: A Macroeconometric Analysis," Department of Economic Analysis and Policy, Reserve Bank of India, Bombay.

Bhide, S., M. Panda, S. Pohit, and D. K. Joshi. 1994. "Analysis of India's Fertilizer Pricing Policies: A CGE Modelling Exercise," mimeo, NCAER, New Delhi.

Bhide, S., A. Sinha, S. Pohit, and D. K. Joshi. 1995. "Macro Modelling for Forecasting and Policy Analysis," Final Report, NCAER, New Delhi (mimeo).

Bhide, Shashanka and Sanjib Pohit. 1993. "Forecasting and Policy Analysis through a CGE Model for India," *Margin*, 25(3), April to June, pp. 271–92.

Brown, Drusilla K., Alan V. Deardorff, and Robert M. Stern. 1993. "Protection and Real Wages: Old and New Trade Theories and Their Empirical Counterparts," Discussion Paper No.331, May 1993, *Research Forum on International Economics,* Institute of Public Policy Studies, University of Michigan, Ann Arbor.

Brown, Drusilla K., Alan V. Deardorff, and Robert M. Stern. 1996. "Computational Analysis of the Economic Effects of an East Asian Preferential Trading Bloc," *Journal of the Japanese and International Economies*, 10, pp. 37–70.

Central Statistical Organization, Government of India. "Input-Output Transaction Table, 1983–84," published by Department of Statistics, Sept. 1990.

Central Statistical Organization, Government of India. "National Accounts Statistics," published by Department of Statistics, Feb. 1993.

Central Statistical Organization, Government of India. "Annual Survey of Industries, Summary Results for Factory Sector," year 1987–88 and 1988–89, published by Department of Statistics.

Chadha, Rajesh, S. Djankov, and Sanjib Pohit. 1995. "Equations for the Michigan Brown-Deardorff-Stern (BDS) CGE Trade Model," *School of Public Policy Studies*, Univ. of Michigan, unpublished mimeo.

Chadha, Rajesh, Sanjib Pohit, and P. L. Bina. 1995. "Capital-Labor Substitution in Indian Industries," presented in *The 31st Annual Conference of the Indian Econometric Society,* National Institute of Bank Management, 12–14th May-1995, Pune, India.

Chadha, Rajesh et al. 1996. "Trade Policy Analysis for Asia and the Pacific Region," NCAER, Report submitted to ESCAP, Bangkok.

Chadha, R., S. Pohit, A. V. Deardorff, and R. M. Stern. 1996a. "The India Model of Production, Trade and Employment," Working Paper No. 64. New Delhi: National Council of Applied Economic Research.

Chadha, R., S. Pohit, A. V. Deardorff, and R. M. Stern. 1996b. "Analysis of India's Reforms: A CGE Modelling Exercise," Working Paper No. 65. New Delhi: National Council of Applied Economic Research.

Chadha, R., S. Pohit, A. V. Deardorff, and R. M. Stern. 1998. "Analysis of India's Policy Reforms, *The World Economy*, 21(2), 235–59.

Chakravarty, S. and R. Eckaus. 1964. "An Approach to a Multisectoral Intertemporal Planning Model" in R.N. Rosenstein (ed.) *Capital Formation and Economic Development*, pp. 110–27, London.

Chakravarty, S. and L. Lefeber. 1965. "An Optimising Planning Model," *The Economic Weekly*, vol. 17, Feb., pp. 237–52.

Cole, S. and G. A. Meagher. 1984. "Growth and Income Distribution in India: A General Equilibrium Analysis," in S. I. Cohen et al. (eds.) *The Modelling of Socio-Economic Planning Processes*, pp. 315–48, Aldershot, Gower.

Deardorff, Alan V. and Robert M. Stern. 1986. *The Michigan Model of World Production and Trade: Theory and Applications*, Cambridge, Mass., MIT Press.

Deardorff, Alan V. and Robert M. Stern. 1990. *Computational Analysis of Global Trading Arrangements*, The University of Michigan Press, Ann Arbor.

DeJanvry, A. and K. Subba Rao. 1986. *Agricultural Price Policy and Income Distribution*, Oxford University Press, New Delhi.

Desai, M. J. 1972. "Macro-econometric Models for India–A Survey," *Sankhya*, Series B, vol. 3, pp. 169–206.

DGCIS, Government of India. "Trade Data on Magnetic Tape," year 1989–90 and 1990–91.

DGCIS, Government of India. "Statistics of the Custom and Excise Revenue Collection of the Indian Union," various issues.

Dixon, P. B., B. R. Paramenter, A. A. Powell, and P. J. Wilcoxen. 1992. *"Notes and Problems in Applied General Equilibrium Economics*, Advanced Textbooks in Economics, no. 32, North-Holland, Amsterdam.

Dixit, Avinash and Joseph E. Stiglitz. 1977. "Monopolistic Competition and Optimum Product Diversity," *American Economic Review,* Volume 67, June, pp. 297–308.

Diwan, R. and R. Kallianpur. 1985. "Biological Technology and Land Productivity: Fertilizer and Food Production," *World Development*, 13, pp. 627–38.

Fertilizer Association of India, "Fertilizer Statistics, 1993–94," New Delhi.

General Agreement on Tariffs and Trade. 1993. *India: Trade Policy Review*, Vol. I and II, GATT, Geneva.

Goldar, B. N. and H. N. Saleem. 1992. "India's Tariff Structure: Effective Rates of Protection of Indian Industries," *Studies in Industrial Development*, Ministry of Industry, Government of India.

Government of India (various issues). Export and Import Policy documents.

Government of India (various issues). *Economic Survey*, Ministry of Finance.

Government of India, Ministry of Finance, Economic Division. *Economic Survey, 1995–96.*

Government of India. 1986. "Discussion Paper on Administered Price Policy," Ministry of Finance, New Delhi.

Government of India, 1991. "Tax Reforms Committee: Interim Report," Chairman: Raja J. Chelliah, Ministry of Finance.

Government of India, 1992. "Tax Reforms Committee: Final Report Part I," Chairman: Raja J. Chelliah, Ministry of Finance.

Government of India, 1993. "Tax Reforms Committee: Final Report Part II," Chairman: Raja J. Chelliah, Ministry of Finance.

Gulati, Ashok, 1998. "Indian Agriculture in an Open Economy: Will it Prosper?" Chapter 6 in *India's Economic Reforms and Development*, Isher Singh Ahluwalia and I.M.D. Little (eds.), Oxford University Press, Delhi.

Gulati, Ashok and Rajesh Chadha. 1995. "India Poised for Take-off? Reforms in Trade, Industry and Agriculture: Stock-Taking and Future Challenges," article published in *Understanding India's Economic Reforms: The Past, The Present, and The Future!*, Vol. 5, eds. Raj Kapila and Uma Kapila, Academic Foundation, Delhi.

Gupta, S. 1983. "India and the Second OPEC Price Shock—An Economy-wide Analysis," *Weltwirtschaftliches Archiv.*, 119, pp. 122–35.

Gupta S. and S. Togan. 1984. "Who benefits from adjustment process in developing countries? A test in India, Kenya and Turkey," *Journal of Policy Modelling*, vol. 6, pp. 95–109.

Helpman, Elhahan and Paul R. Krugman, 1985. *Market Structure and Foreign Trade: Increasing Returns, Imperfect Competition, and the International Economy*, The MIT Press, Cambridge.

Human Development Report, UNDP, 1996.

Hussain, Abid (Chairman). 1984. "Report of the Committee on Trade Policies," Ministry of Commerce, Government of India.

IEG – DSE Research Team. 1994. "A New Econometric Model for India," Institute of Economic Growth, September (mimeo).

Jadhav, N. 1990. "Monetary Modelling of Indian Economy: A Survey," *Reserve Bank of India Occasional Papers*, vol. 11, no. 2, pp. 83–152.

Jayaraman, T. K. 1977. "Import Demand Functions of India," *Foreign Trade Review*, 11(4), pp. 362–67.

Joshi D. K., S. Bhide, A. Kapoor, and R. Satish. 1995. "Medium-Term Assessment of the Indian Economy through a Macroeconometric Model," *Margin*, vol. 27, no. 3, April–June, pp. 257–324.

Joshi, Vijay and I.M.D. Little. 1994. *India: Macroeconomics and Political Economy 1964–1991*, Oxford University Press, Delhi.

Kelkar, V. L. and Kumar, R. 1990. "Industrial Growth in the Eighties: Emerging Policy Issues," *Economic and Political Weekly,* Jan. 27.

Keuschnigg, Christian and Wilhelm Kohler. 1996. "Dynamics of Trade Liberalization," in Joseph F. Francois and Kenneth A. Reinert (eds.), *Ap-*

plied Methods for Trade Policy Analysis, Cambridge University Press, New York.

Krishna, K. L. 1997. "Industrial Growth and Diversification," in Uma Kapila (ed.), *Indian Economy Since Independence,* 1997–98 edition, pp. 650–73.

Krishna, K. L., K. Krishnamurthy, V. N. Pandit, and P. D. Sharma. 1991. "Macro-econometric Modelling in India: A Selective Review of Research, " *Development Paper*, no. 9, ESCAP, UN, New York.

Krishnamurthy, K. 1964. "An Econometric Model of India, 1948–61." Ph.D. Dissertation (Unpublished), University of Pennsylvania.

Krishnamurthy, K. 1985. "Inflation and Growth – A Model for India," in K. Krishnamurthy and V. N. Pandit (eds.), *Macro-economic Model of the Indian Economy*, Hindustan Publishing Corporation, Delhi.

Krishnamurthy K. 1992. "Status of Macro Modelling in India," Paper presented in the Workshop on Macro Modelling in Forecasting and Policy Analysis, Ottawa, Canada.

Krishnamurthy, K., V. Pandit, and P. D. Sharma. 1989. "Parameters of Growth in a Developing Mixed Economy: The Indian Experience," *Journal of Quantitative Economics*, vol. 5, pp. 295–325.

Lucas, R.E.B. 1988. "Demand for India's Manufactured Exports," *Journal of Development Economics,* 29, pp. 63–75.

Mac Mohan, Garry. 1989. "Computable General Equilibrium Modelling: A Survey with Reference to India," *The India Economic Journal*, vol. 37, pp. 1–14.

Madhur, S. 1987. "Forecasts and Policy Evaluations Using a Macro-econometric Model for India," presented at Model Comparison Conference at National Central University, Taiwan, May 25–27 (mimeo).

Mahalanobis, P. C. 1953. "Some Observations on the Process of Growth of National Income," *Sankhya,* vol. 12, no.4, pp. 307–12.

Mallick, S. K. and T. K. Kumar. 1995. "A Non-econometric Review of Indian Macro-economic Models," *Artha Vijnana*, March, vol.37, no.1, pp. 1–45.

Mammen, T. 1967. "*An Econometric study of the Money Market in India*," Ph.D. Dissertation, (Unpublished), University of Pennsylvania.

Manne, A. S. and A. Rudra. 1965. "A Consistency Model for India's Fourth Plan." *Sankhya*, series B, vol.27, pp. 557–144.

Martin, Will and L. Alan Winters (eds.). 1996. *The Uruguay Round and the Developing Countries*, Cambridge University Press, London.

Marwah, K., 1964. "An Econometric Model of Price Behaviour in India," Ph.D. Thesis submitted to the University of Pennsylvania.

Marwah, K. 1991. "Macro Econometric Modelling of South East Asia: The Case of India," in R. G. Bodkin, L. B. Klein, and K. Marwah (eds.), *A History of Macro Economic Model Building*. Edward Elgar, UK.

Ministry of Agriculture, Government of India. "Cost of Principal Crops in India," year 1991.

Ministry of Commerce, Government of India. "Export-Import Policy," April 1987 – March 1990.

Ministry of Finance, Government of India. "Budget of the Central Government," year 1991–92.

Ministry of Finance, Government of India. "Economic Survey," year 1991–92.

Ministry of Railways, Government of India. "Annual Report and Accounts 1990–91, Indian Railways."

Mohan, Rakesh. 1977. *Development, Structural Change and Urbanization: Explorations With A Three Sector General Equilibrium Model Applied to India*, Ph.D. Dissertation, Princeton University, New Jersey.

Mohan, Rakesh. 1992. "Industrial Policy and Controls," in Bimal Jalan (ed.), *The Indian Economy: Problems and Prospects*, Viking, New Delhi.

Narayana, N.S.S., K. S. Parikh, and T. N. Srinivasan. 1987. "Indian Agricultural Policy: An Applied General Equilibrium Model," *Journal of Policy Modelling*, vol. 9, pp. 527–58.

Narayana, N. S., K. S. Parikh, and T. N. Srinivasan. 1991. *Agricultural Growth and Redistribution of Incomes Model,* North Holland / Allied Publishers.

Narsimhan, M. (Chairman). 1985. "Report of the Committee to Examine the Principles of a Possible Shift from Physical to Financial Controls," Government of India.

Panda M. K. and H. Sarkar. 1990. Resource Mobilisation through Administered Prices in an Indian CGE Model," in Lance Taylor (ed.), *Socially Relevant Policy Analysis: Structuralist Computable General Equilibrium Models for the Developing World,* Cambridge: MIT Press.

Panda, M. K. and H. Sarkar. 1991. "Analysis of Fiscal Squeeze through a Structuralist CGE Model," *Margin* 23:239–55.

Pandit, V. 1994. "A Note on the Structural Macroeconomic Model of India," Delhi School of Economics, mimeo.

Pandit, V. 1986. "Price Adjustments and India's Trade Performance: A Macro Economic Analysis," presented to the fall meeting of the Project Link, Bangkok.

Pani, P. K. 1977. *A Macro Economic Model Of India*. Macmillan, Delhi.

Pani, P. K. 1984. "A Macro Model of Indian Economy with Specific Reference to Output Demand and Prices, 1969–70 to 1981–82," *RBI Occasional Papers*, vol. no.2, pp. 113–239, December.

Patra, D. and R. Ranjan. 1992. "The Structure of India's Imports: 1970–71 to 1988–89," Reserve Bank of India, *Occasional Papers*, vol. 13, no. 2, June pp. 81–97.

Planning Commission, Government of India. 1973. "A Technical Note on the Approach to the Fifth Plan of India, 1974–79," Prospective Planning Division, Government of India, New Delhi.

Planning Commission, Government of India. "A Technical Note to the 8th Plan of India (1992–97)".

Planning Commission, Government of India. "A Technical Note to the 7th Plan of India (1985–90)" .

Pohit, Sanjib and Shashanka Bhide. 1994. "Demand Factors of India's Exports," NCAER, mimeo.

Pohit, Sanjib and Shashanka Bhide. 1994. "Demand Factors of India's Imports," NCAER, mimeo.

Pradhan, B. D., D. K. Rath, and A. Sharma. 1990. "Complementarity between Public and Private Investment in India," *Journal of Development Economics*, vol. 33, no. 1, pp. 101–116.

Pursell, G. 1996. "Indian Trade Policies Since The 1991/92 Reforms," *Draft, July 25, 1996,* International Trade Department, World Bank.

Quizon, J. B. and H. P. Binswanger. 1986. "Modelling the Impact of Agricultural Growth and Government Policy on Income Distribution in India.," *The World Bank Economic Review*, vol. 1, no.1, pp. 103–148.

Rangarajan, C. and R. R. Arif. 1990. "Money, Output and Prices: A Macroeconometric Model," *Economic and Political Weekly*, vol.25, pp. 837–52.

Rao, Narahari. 1985. *Exchange Rate and Commercial Policy in a Controlled Trade Regime, A Case Study of India*, Oxford University Press.

Rastogi, A. B. 1991. "A Rational Expectation Model of the Indian Economy," Working Paper no. 91/102, Department of Economics and Accounting, University of Liverpool.

Ratha, K. and A. Sahoo. 1990. "India's Exports of Capital Goods," *Economic and Political Weekly,* Aug. 25, pp. 1897–1903.

Rattso, J. 1987. "The Macroeconomic Performance in India 1980–85: An Applied General Equilibrium Analysis," *Journal of Quantitative Economics*, 3, 225–58.

Rattso, J. 1988. "Macro-dynamic Adjustment Mechanisms in India," *World Development*, 16:959–73.

Ray, A. K. 1989. "Indian Plan Models: A Review," *RBI Occasional Papers*, pp. 315–30.

Sandee. J. 1960. "A Demonstration Planning Model for India," *Indian Statistical Institute Series no.7,* Statistical Publishing Society, Calcutta.

Sarkar, S. and S. V. Subbarao. 1981. "A Short Term Macro Forecasting Model for India: Structure and Uses," *Indian Economic Review*, 16:55–80.

Sarkar, H. and M. K. Panda. 1989. "A Short Term Structural Macro-economic Model for India: Applications to Policy Analysis," in Econometric Modelling and Forecasting in Asia, Development Paper no. 9, ESCAP, UN, New York.

Sinha, N. 1986. *A Structural Model for Indian Economy*, R.B.S.A. Publisher, Jaipur.

Srinivasan T. N. 1997. "Foreign Trade Policies and Indian Development ," Chapter 46 in *Indian Economy since Independence*, ed. Uma Kapila, Academic Foundation, Delhi.

Srivastava, D. K. 1981. "Policy Simulations, with a Macro-econometric Model of the Indian Economy," *Journal of Policy Modelling*, vol. 3, no. 3, pp. 37–395.

Stern, Robert M., Alan V. Deardorff, and Drusilla K. Brown. 1992. *A U.S.–Mexico–Canada Free Trade Agreement: Sectoral Employment Effects and Regional/ Occupational Employment Realignments in the United States*, Report to the National Commission for Employment Policy, Washington, D.C.

Storm, Servaas. 1995. Macroeconomic Impact of Agricultural Price Policy: A CGE Model for India, mimeo.

Subramanium, S. 1993. "Agricultural Trade Liberalization in India," Development Center Studies, Organisation for Economic Cooperation and Development, Paris.

Taylor, L. 1983. *Structuralist Macroeconomics: Applicable Models for the Third World*, New York: Basic Books.

Tendulkar, Suresh D. 1981. "Indian Development Strategy: Compulsions and Constraints," *Working Paper No. 231*, Delhi School Of Economics, Delhi.

University of Michigan. "Michigan Database," Ann Arbor, USA.

Virmani, Arvind. 1994. "Demand and Supply Factors in India's Trade," *Economic and Political Weekly,* Feb. 9, pp. 311–14.

Yang, Xiaokai and J. Heijdra. 1993. "Monopolistic Competition and Optimum Product Diversity: Comment," *American Economic Review,* 83, pp. 295–301.

Whalley, J. 1975. "How Reliable is Partial Equilibrium Analysis?" *Review of Economics and Statistics*, 57, pp. 299–310.

World Bank. 1989. *India: An Industrializing Economy in Transition*, A World Bank Country Study.

World Bank. 1993. *The East Asian Miracle: Economic Growth and Public Policy*, Oxford University Press, Oxford.

Appendix 1

EQUATIONS OF THE INDIA CGE MODEL AND SECTORAL CLASSIFICATIONS

COUNTRY EQUATIONS

A. Final Demand

Final demand equations for various sectors are derived assuming that all households share a common Cobb-Douglas utility function as specified in function (I):[1]

$$U = \prod_{j \in ALS} C_j^{\alpha_j} \qquad \text{(I)}$$

At this first stage, expenditure is allocated across goods without regard for the country of origin or the producing firm. Final demand equations for different sectors are obtained by maximizing the above utility function subject to household income E.[2] Equation (1) gives the (changes in logarithms of) final demands for all the 34 sectors of the Indian economy.

$$\hat{C}_j = \hat{E} - \hat{P}_j \qquad j \in ALS \qquad (1)$$

A constant fraction of the budget is spent on each good since we have assumed a Cobb-Douglas utility function. The per cent change in the demand for a good is therefore the difference between the per cent changes in expenditure and price.

B. Intermediate Demand

To state demands for intermediate inputs from different industries and primary inputs, we assume a Leontief production function of the form given in function (II):

$$S_k = \min\left[\frac{n_k V_k}{v_{ko}}, \frac{Z_{1k}}{v_{1k}}, \frac{Z_{2k}}{v_{2k}}, \frac{Z_{3k}}{v_{3k}}, \ldots, \frac{Z_{34k}}{v_{34k}}\right] - S_k^o \qquad k \in ALS \qquad \text{(II)}$$

From (II), the change in intermediate demand for input j by sector k is given in equation (2). That is, it is assumed that all intermediate inputs are required in fixed proportions to production. The demand for each intermediate input is thus proportional to production. For example, if output in sector k rises by 5 per cent, then the use of every single intermediate input from each of the 34 sectors must also rise by 5 per cent.

$$\hat{Z}_{jk} = \hat{S}_k \qquad j,k \in ALS \qquad (2)$$

C. Total Demand

Total demand for goods is given in equation (3). To obtain total demand we begin with household demand for good *j*. In addition, we must also add intermediate demand for good *j* by all the *k* different sectors. In terms of per cent change, the total change in demand for good *j* is a weighted average of the per cent changes in final and intermediate demands for good *j*.

$$\hat{D}_j = v_{j0}\hat{C}_j + \sum_{k\in ALS} vd_{jk}\hat{Z}_{jk} \qquad j \in ALS \qquad (3)$$

D. Product Demand

Aggregates of industry demands are defined identically for both final and intermediate demands as follows:

a) For tradable sectors under perfect competition, state monopoly and administered prices, we have the Armington function (III):

$$Z_{jk} = \left[Z_{I_{jk}}^{\rho_j} + Z_{W_{jk}}^{\rho_j}\right]^{\frac{1}{\rho_j}} \qquad j \in TPCS \cup TSMS \cup TICSAP,\ k \in ALS \qquad \text{(III)}$$

According to the Armington assumption, products are differentiated by country of origin. In this model, the countries are India and rest-of-world (ROW).

b) For tradable sectors under monopolistic competition, we have the Dixit-Stiglitz function (IV):

$$Z_{jk} = \left[\sum_{m=1}^{n_j} Z_{I_{mjk}}^{\rho_j} + Z_{W_{jk}}^{\rho_j}\right]^{\frac{1}{\rho_j}} \qquad j \in TICS,\ k \in ALS \qquad \text{(IV)}$$

where m stands for firms in India.

Following Dixit and Stiglitz (1977), products are differentiated by firm under monopolistic competition. In our model, products are differentiated by firm in India along with one more variety entering from ROW. Total demand for tradable good *j* is then broken down into the various import and domestic varieties of good *j*. First, total demand is allocated between *imports* as given in equation (4) and a *typical domestically produced variety* as given in equation (5). We assume that the number of firms remains unchanged in nine perfectly competitive sectors (sectors 1 to 4 and 29 to 34 excluding 31), four public sector monopolies (sectors 16, 20, 27, 28) and three imperfectly competitive price administered sectors (sectors 12, 14, 21).

$$\hat{D}_j^m = \hat{D}_j + \sigma_j\theta_j^I(\hat{P}_j^I - \hat{P}_j^M) - \frac{\sigma_j\theta_j^I}{\sigma_j - 1}\hat{n}_j \qquad j \in TRS \qquad (4)$$

$$\hat{D}_j^I = \hat{D}_j + \sigma_j\theta_j^M(\hat{P}_j^M - \hat{P}_j^I) - \frac{\sigma_j\theta_j^I}{\sigma_j - 1}\hat{n}_j \qquad j \in TRS \qquad (5)$$

The last term in equations (4) and (5) vanishes for $j \in TPCS \cup TSMS \cup TICSAP$ since $\hat{n}_j = 0$.

As can be seen from the first terms in both equations, the first determinant of import demand and domestic demand is total demand. Assuming that the number of firms and relative prices do not change, if total demand rises for example by 5 per cent then import and domestic demand will each also rise by 5 per cent.

Of course, if relative prices do change, then consumers will reallocate between imports and the domestic variety. If the price of the domestic variety rises relative to imports, then consumers will certainly substitute away from the domestic good toward imports, as can be seen from the second term in each of the two equations. How much substitution takes place depends on the elasticity of substitution, σ. The higher is σ, the more sensitive consumers are to the change in relative prices.

Another force affecting demand for the import aggregate and each of the domestic varieties is the number of domestic firms. As the number of domestic firms rises, the demand for each incumbent firm will fall and demand for the import aggregate will also fall as noted in equations (4) and (5). That effect is absent in the case of sectors for which $\hat{n}_j = 0$.

E. Prices

There are various price relationships that must hold in the model, including one that is merely definitional as given in equation (6). Equation (7) specifies that the per cent changes in prices of domestic varieties as well as the rupee price of the imported variety in the sectors under administered prices are simply equal to the corresponding changes in their administered prices.

$$\hat{P}_j = \theta_j^I \hat{P}_j^I + \theta_j^M \hat{P}_j^M - \frac{\theta_j^I}{\sigma_j - 1}\hat{n}_j \qquad j \in TRS \tag{6}$$

$$\left.\begin{aligned} \hat{P}_j &= \hat{P}_j^0 & j &\in NTS \\ \hat{P}_j^I &= \hat{P}_j^0 & j &\in TAPS \\ \hat{P}_j^M &= \hat{P}_j^0 & j &\in TAPS \end{aligned}\right\} \tag{7}$$

The last term in equation (6) vanishes for $j \cup TPCS \cup TSMS \cup TICSAP$ since $\hat{n}_j = 0$. It may be observed that the number of varieties enters negatively in equation (6). As the number of varieties rises, the price index falls. This is because consumers like variety. The greater the number of firms, the more variety is available to consumers. Therefore, consumers can achieve a certain level of utility at a lower cost if more varieties are available. Thus, whereas $\hat{P}_j^I$ is the change in price of a physical unit of good j produced in India, $\hat{P}_j^I - \hat{n}_j/(\sigma_j - 1)$ is the price of acquiring a unit of utility from the varieties of goods produced in India. P_j^M and P_j are similarly defined in terms of utility.

The sensitivity of the price index to the number of varieties depends on the elasticity of substitution. The lower is σ, the more the price index falls when new varieties are introduced. A low σ implies that varieties are very different from one another; that is, addition of a new variety brings much additional value to the consumer. Thus, there is a large decline in the implicit cost of achieving a particular level of utility from consumption.

The next two equations, (8) and (9), link world prices to domestic prices. Equation (8) simply states that the landed price of imports from rest of the world is determined by the world price of goods produced abroad, the exchange rate (rupees per dollar) and the tariff equivalent. Equation (9) states that the domestic price of a typical variety is determined by the domestic currency equivalent of the price at which India exports to the world markets.

$$\hat{P}_j^M = \hat{P}_{Wj}^W + \hat{R} + \hat{t}_j^{Meq} \qquad j \in TRS \tag{8}$$

$$\hat{P}_{Wj}^I = \hat{P}_j^I - \hat{R} + \hat{t}_j^{Xeq} \qquad j \in TRS \tag{9}$$

Equation (10) relates to the sectors under perfect competition. The price of each of these sectors must be equal to marginal cost inclusive of the net production tax. Equation (11) states that the percent change in price of a domestic variety for tradable public sector monopolies must be equal to marginal cost inclusive of net production tax. Equation (12) specifies that per cent changes in the prices of nontraded sectors under administered prices are equal to the sum of corresponding changes in their administered prices and the premium duc to supply shortages.

$$\hat{P}_j^I = \hat{MC}_j \qquad j \in TPCS \tag{10}$$

$$\hat{P}_j^I = \hat{MC}_j \qquad j \in TSMS \tag{11}$$

$$\hat{P}_j^I = \hat{MC}_j + \hat{PR}_j \qquad j \in NSMS \tag{12}$$

Equation (13) states that price must be equal to total cost for sectors under imperfect competition.

$$\hat{P}_j^I = \theta_j^{MC}\hat{MC}_j + \theta_j^{FC}(\hat{p}_j^V + \hat{n}_j - \hat{S}_j) \qquad j \in TICS \tag{13}$$

$$\hat{n}_j = 0 \qquad j \in TICSAP$$

Imperfectly competitive firms in sectors in which entry occurs must also charge the optimal mark-up over marginal cost, inclusive of net production tax. As stated in equation (14), the optimal mark-up depends on the elasticity of demand. The higher the elasticity (in absolute value), the smaller the gap between price and marginal cost.

$$\hat{P}_j^I = \hat{MC}_j + \frac{\hat{\eta}_j}{\eta_j + 1} \qquad j \in TMCS \tag{14}$$

Finally, the price of the primary inputs aggregate (value added) is given in equation (15). For all the sectors except the four agricultural sectors, this price is the cost-share-weighted average of the returns to primary inputs, capital and labor. However, in the case of the four agricultural sectors, the price of the primary inputs aggregate is given in equation (16) as a weighted average of the returns to the capital-land composite and the wage rate. Equation (17) gives the price of the capital-land composite.

$$\hat{P}_j^V = \theta_{j1}^L \hat{w} + \theta_{j1}^K \hat{r}_j \qquad j \in (TAGS)^C \qquad (15)$$

$$\hat{P}_j^V = \theta_{j2}^{KF} \hat{P}_j^{KF} + \theta_{j2}^L \hat{w} \qquad j \in TAGS \qquad (16)$$

$$\hat{P}_j^{KF} = \theta_{j3}^k \hat{r}_j + \theta_{j3}^F \hat{f} \qquad j \in TAGS \qquad (17)$$

$$\hat{r}_j = \hat{r} \qquad j \in (SMS)^C$$

F. Marginal Cost and Average Cost

There are two components of marginal cost as noted in equation (18). The first term is the cost of primary inputs (capital and labor, and land as an additional factor in agricultural sectors), and the second term is the intermediate inputs from all of the goods sectors.

$$\hat{MC}_j = b_{j0} \frac{\theta_j^{VK}}{\theta_j^{MC}} \hat{P}_j^V + \sum_{k \in ALS} \frac{b_{kj}}{\theta_j^{MC}} \hat{P}_k + bt_j \hat{NT}_j \qquad j \in ALS \qquad (18)$$

where $\theta_i^{VK} = \theta_i^{MC} = 1$ for $j \in TPCS \cup TSMS \cup NTS$

It is worth pointing out here the nature of technology. As will be seen later, marginal cost is made up of the cost of labor, capital and intermediate inputs. However, labor and capital are the only fixed inputs. No intermediate inputs are required for fixed costs. The cost of fixed labor and capital inputs is captured by P_j^V given in the first term on the right-hand side of equation (18).

G. Demand for Primary Inputs

Aggregates of industry demands for primary inputs are given in functions (V), (VI), and (VII):

$$V_j = \left[L_j^{\rho_j^1} + K_j^{\rho_j^1} \right]^{\frac{1}{\rho_j^1}} \qquad j \in (TAGS)^C \qquad (V)$$

$$V_j = \left[L_j^{\rho_j^2} + KF_j^{\rho_j^2} \right]^{\frac{1}{\rho_j^2}} \qquad j \in TAGS \qquad (VI)$$

$$KF_j = \left[K_j^{\rho_j^3} + F_j^{\rho_j^3} \right]^{\frac{1}{\rho_j^3}} \qquad j \in TAGS \qquad (VII)$$

Capital and labor are combined to form a primary input aggregate in the case of all sectors except the four agricultural sectors where we consider land to be an additional primary factor of production. The primary input aggregate is then used in fixed proportion to firm output. This is shown in equation (19) for a representative firm under imperfect competition. Equation (20) corresponds to all other sectors, including nine sectors under perfect competition and five public monopoly sectors.

$$\hat{V}_j = \hat{S}_j - \hat{n}_j \qquad j \in TMCS \tag{19}$$

$$\hat{V}_j = \hat{S}_j \qquad j \in (TMCS)^C \tag{20}$$

Once the demand for the primary inputs aggregate has been determined, expenditure is then allocated between capital and labor for all sectors except agriculture, in which land is an additional primary factor. This is given in equation (21). Return to capital is the same for sectors across which capital is mobile but is sector specific for sectors in which it is immobile.

$$\hat{L}_j = \theta_j^{VK}\hat{V}_j - \overline{\sigma}_{j1}\theta_{j1}^{k}(\hat{w} - \hat{r}_j) + \hat{n}_j \qquad j \in (TAGS)^C \tag{21}$$

$$\hat{n}_j = 0 \qquad j \in SMS \cup TNAGS \cup TICSAP$$

$$\theta_j^{VK} = 1 \qquad j \in TNAGS \cup NSMS$$

$$\hat{r}_j = \hat{r} \qquad j \in TMCS \cup TICSAP \cup TNAGS$$

For sectors j = 1...4 (TAGS), we use the separate labor demand function in equation (25) below.

The demand for capital, in all sectors except agriculture, is given in equation (22), which is analogous to equation (21) for labor demand. As noted in equation (23), it is assumed that the capital stock remains fixed for the five public monopoly sectors (four tradable and one nontraded). In these sectors, (22) serves to determine the sector-specific return to capital, r_j.

$$\hat{K}_j = \theta_j^{VK}\hat{V}_j + \overline{\sigma}_{j1}\theta_{j1}^{L}(\hat{w} - \hat{r}_j) + \hat{n}_j \qquad j \in (TAGS)^C \tag{22}$$

$$\hat{n}_j = 0 \qquad j \in SMS \cup TNAGS \cup TICSAP$$

$$\theta_j^{VK} = 1 \qquad j \in TNAGS \cup NSMS$$

$$\hat{r}_j = \hat{r} \qquad j \in TMCS \cup TICSAP \cup TNAGS$$

$$\hat{K}_j = 0 \qquad j \in SMS \tag{23}$$

For sectors j = 1...4 (TAGS), we use the separate capital demand function in equation (26) below.

As already mentioned, we assume that land is an additional primary factor of production, apart from capital and labor, in the case of the four agricultural sectors. The primary inputs aggregate is a CES function of labor and a composite of land and capital. The land-capital composite is, in turn, a CES function of land and capital. The demand for the land-capital composite, as given in equation (24), depends on the demand for the primary inputs aggregate and the relative price of labor and the land-capital composite. Equation (25) provides the corresponding demand for labor. Equations (26) and (27) provide demands for capital and land, respectively, each depending on the land-capital composite and relative prices of capital and land.

$$\hat{K}F_j = \hat{V}_j - \overline{\sigma}_{j2}\theta^L_{j2}(\hat{P}^{KF}_j - \hat{w}) \qquad j \in TAGS \qquad (24)$$

$$\hat{L}_j = \hat{V}_j + \overline{\sigma}_{j2}\theta^{KF}_{j2}(\hat{P}^{KF}_j - \hat{w}) \qquad j \in TAGS \qquad (25)$$

$$\hat{K}_j = \hat{K}F_j - \overline{\sigma}_{j3}\theta^F_{j3}(\hat{r}_j - \hat{f}) \qquad j \in TAGS \qquad (26)$$

$$\hat{F}_j = \hat{K}F_j + \overline{\sigma}_{j3}\theta^K_{j3}(\hat{r}_j - \hat{f}) \qquad j \in TAGS \qquad (27)$$

$$\hat{r}_j = \hat{r} \qquad j \in TMCS \cup TICSAP \cup TNAGS$$

H. Nontradable Goods Market Equilibrium

Market clearing in the nontradable rail transport sector requires that domestic demand equals domestic supply, as given in equation (28).

$$\hat{S}_j = \hat{D}_j \qquad j \in NTS \qquad (28)$$

I. Demand Elasticity

The demand elasticity for tradable goods under imperfect competition is given in equation (29). The demand curve will be perceived as more elastic if the number of competing firms rises or the world prices of competing goods fall relative to the domestic goods.

$$\hat{\eta}_j = \frac{(\sigma_j - 1)}{\eta_j n_j}\theta^I_j\left(\hat{D}^I_j + \hat{P}^I_j - \hat{P}_j - \hat{D}_j\right) \qquad j \in TMCS \qquad (29)$$

J. Primary Factors Market Equilibrium

Capital, labor and land markets clear when the sum over industry demand for each factor equals an exogenous supply. The relevant factor market equilibrium conditions are given in equations (30), (31) and (32), respectively.

$$\sum_{j \in ALS} h^K_j \hat{K}_j = \hat{K}^0 \qquad (30)$$

$$\sum_{j \in ALS} h^L_j \hat{L}_j = \hat{L}^0 \qquad (31)$$

$$\sum_{j \in TAGS} h^F_j \hat{F}_j = \hat{F}^0 \qquad (32)$$

where h^K_j, h^L_j and h^F_j are the fractions of *K*, *L* and *F*, respectively, employed in industry *j*.

K. Nontariff Barriers

There are two types of trade barrier that affect imports, nominal tariffs and quantitative restrictions (QRs), i.e., nontariff barriers (NTBs). Each QR is captured by an endogenous tariff equivalent. The tariff equivalent is calculated endogenously in the model so that, if demand or supply conditions change, then the tariff equivalent will also change to hold the quantity demanded constant.

The actual tariff that applies is then composed of the nominal tariff (first term in equation (33)) and the tariff equivalent of the NTB (second term). The QRs are invoked by specifying the fraction of the sector covered by NTBs, θ_j^{MQ}, and the desired change in the QRs, $\hat{Q}_j^M$, as in equation (33). Export taxes and quantitative restrictions are treated similarly in equation (34), which specifies the export tax equivalent imposed by India on exports to ROW.

$$\hat{t}_j^{Meq} = \hat{t}_j + (\hat{D}_j^M - \hat{Q}_j^M)\frac{\theta_j^{MQ}}{\sigma_j(1-\theta_j^{MQ})} \qquad (33)$$

$$j \in TMCS \cup TNAGS \cup TAGSNA$$

$$\hat{t}_j^{Xeq} = \hat{t}_j^X + (\hat{D}_{jR} - \hat{Q}_j^X)\frac{\theta_j^{XQ}}{\eta_j^R(1-\theta_j^{XQ})} \qquad j \in TRS \qquad (34)$$

Equation (35) specifies that the domestic price of the "food" sector is taken as numeraire and is therefore constant.

$$\hat{P}_5^I = 0 \qquad (35)$$

L. Demand for India's Exports to ROW:

The export demand for a tradable good from India to ROW depends on India's price and the demand elasticity for India's exports. This is given in equation (36) for all tradable sectors.

$$\hat{D}_{jR}^I = \eta_j^R \hat{P}_{Wj}^I \qquad j \in TRS \qquad (36)$$

M. Trade Balance

The trade balance (in dollars) is the sum over changes in the value of exports less changes in the value of imports. This is given in equation (37).

$$\Delta B^T = \sum_{j \in TRS} D_{jR}^I P_{Wj}^I (\hat{D}_{jR}^I + \hat{P}_{Wj}^I) - \sum_{j \in TRS} D_j^M P_{Wj}^W (\hat{D}_j^M + \hat{P}_{Wj}^W) \qquad (37)$$

N. Tradable Goods Market Equilibrium

The market for each tradable good in India requires that total supply should be equal to total world demand. Total world demand includes demand originating in India plus that in ROW. This is given in equation (38).

$$S_j\hat{S}_j = D^I_{jR}\hat{D}^I_{jR} + D^I_j n_j(\hat{D}^I_j + \hat{n}_j) \qquad j \in TRS \tag{38}$$

$$\hat{n}_j = 0 \qquad j \in TPCS \cup TSMS \cup TICSAP$$

$$n_j = 1 \qquad j \in TPCS \cup TSMS$$

O. Exchange Rate

Exchange rates are determined in equations (39) and (40), with separate cases for fixed and flexible exchange rate regimes. If we consider India to be on a pegged exchange rate system, equation (39) sets it exogenously with respect to the U.S. dollar. But if India adopts a flexible exchange rate, equation (40) determines it by the requirement that the balance of trade plus an exogenous capital inflow be equal to zero.

$$\hat{R} = \hat{R}^0 \tag{39}$$

$$\Delta B^T + \Delta B^{K0} = 0 \tag{40}$$

LIST OF EXOGENOUS VARIABLES OF THE MODEL

B^{K0} : Exogenous level of capital inflow into India
F^0 : Supply of agricultural land in India
K^0 : Capital stock in India
K_j : Fixed capital stock in sector *j* ($j \in SMS$)
L^0 : Labor supply in India
NT_j : Net production tax on good *j* ($j \in ALS$)
P^W_{Wj} : World price of good *j* ($j \in TRS$)
Q^M_j : Quota restriction on imports of good *j* by India ($j \in TRS$)
Q^X_j : Restriction on exports of good *j* by India ($j \in TRS$)
S^0_j : Fixed cost parameter in industry *j* ($j \in ALS$)
R^0 : Exogenous level of exchange rate in rupees per U.S. dollar

t_j : One plus tariff imposed by India on imports of good *j* ($j \in TRS$)
t_j^X : One plus tax imposed by India on exports of good *j* (j ∈ TRS)
n_j : Number of firms in industry *j* in India ($j \in TSMS \cup TICSAP \cup TPCS$)

LIST OF ENDOGENOUS VARIABLES

B^T : India's trade balance
C_j : Final demand for good *j* in India ($j \in ALS$)
n_j : Number of firms in industry *j* in India ($j \in TMCS$)
D_j : Total demand for good *j* in India ($j \in ALS$)
D_{jR}^I : Demand in India for good *j* produced by ROW($j \in TRS$)
D_j^I : Demand in India for the good produced by a representative firm in industry *j* in India ($j \in TRS$)
D_j^M : Total demand for imports of good *j* in India ($j \in TRS$)
E : Aggregate nominal expenditure
η_j : Perceived elasticity of demand by a representative firm in industry *j* in India ($j \in TMCS$)
F_j : Demand for land in sector *j* in India ($j \in TAGS$)
f : Return to land in India
K_j : Demand for capital in industry *j* in India ($j \in SMS^C$)
KF_j : Demand for aggregate of land and capital in sector *j* ($j \in TAGS$)
L_j : Demand for labor in industry *j* in India ($j \in ALS$)
MC_j: Marginal cost in India of industry *j* or of a representative firm in industry *j* ($j \in ALS$)
P_j^M : Price index of imported good *j* in India ($j \in TRS$)

P_j^I : Price of domestic good produced by a representative firm in industry *j* in India ($j \in TRS$)
P_j : Price index of good *j* in India ($j \in ALS$)
P_j^0 : Administered price of good *j* ($j \in APS$)
P_{Wj}^I : World price of good *j* produced in India ($j \in TRS$)
P_j^V : Price index of primary input aggregate (i.e., labor and capital or labor and composite of land and capital) in industry *j* in India ($j \in ALS$)
P_j^{KF} : Price index of first-stage primary input aggregate (i.e., labor and composite of capital and land) in sector *j* in India ($j \in TAGS$)
PR_j : Premium over price in industry *j*($j \in NSMS$)
r : Return to capital in India in equilibrium
r_j : Return to capital in India in industry *j* ($j \in ALS$)
R : Exchange rate of rupee per U.S. dollar
S_k : Production of good *k* in India ($k \in ALS$)

t_j^{Meq}: One plus tariff equivalent in industry j imposed by India on imports from ROW ($j \in TRS$)
t_j^{Xeq}: One plus export tax equivalent imposed in industry j by India ($j \in TRS$)
V_j : Primary input aggregate demanded by a representative firm in industry j in India ($j \in ALS$)
w : Wage paid to labor
Z_{jk} : Aggregate of sectoral inputs from industry j into industry k (aggregation of industries and/or firms) ($j,k \in ALS$)
Z_{Ijk}: Intermediate demand for tradable good j of Indian origin by industry k in India ($j \in TPCS \cup TSMS$, $k \in ALS$)
Z_{Wjk}: Intermediate demand for tradable good j of ROW origin by industry k in India ($j \in TPCS \cup TSMS$, $k \in ALS$)
Z_{Imjk}: Intermediate demand for tradable good j of Indian origin by a representative firm in industry k in India ($j \in TICS$, $k \in ALS$)

LIST OF PARAMETERS OF THE MODEL

α_j: Fraction of budget spent on good j ($j \in ALS$)
b_{j0} : Primary input share of total cost in industry j in India ($j \in ALS$)
b_{jk} : Intermediate input k's share of total cost of production in industry j in India ($j\ k \in ALS$)
bt_j : Tax share of total cost in industry j in India ($j \in ALS$)
h_j^K : Fraction of capital in India employed in industry j ($j \in ALS$)
h_j^L : Fraction of labor in India employed in industry j ($j \in ALS$)
h_j^F : Fraction of land in India allocated to sector j ($j \in TAGS$)
v_{j0} : Primary inputs (value-added) per unit output of good j ($j \in ALS$)
v_{jk} : Intermediate demand for good j per unit output of industry k ($j,k \in ALS$)
v_{j0} : Final consumption share of total purchases of good j in India ($j \in ALS$)
vd_{jk} : Intermediate demand for good j by industry k share of purchases of good j in India (j, $k \in ALS$)
θ_j^M : Fraction of expenditure on good j in India devoted to imports ($j \in TRS$)
θ_j^I : Fraction of expenditure on good j in India devoted to goods produced in India ($j \in TRS$)
θ_j^{MQ} : Fraction of imports of goods j by India that are subject to quantitative restriction ($j \in TRS$)
θ_j^{XQ} : Fraction of exports in industry j that are subject to quantitative restriction ($j \in TRS$)
θ_j^{MC} : Variable input share of total cost in industry j in India ($j \in ALS$)
θ_j^{FC} : Fixed cost share of total cost in industry j in India ($j \in TICS$)

θ^{L}_{j1} : Labor's share of expenditure on primary inputs in industry j in India ($j \in TAGS^{C}$)

θ^{L}_{j2} : Labor's share of expenditure on first-stage aggregate of primary inputs in sector j in India ($j \in TAGS$)

θ^{KF}_{j2} : Composite of land and capital's share of expenditure on first-stage aggregate of primary inputs in sector j in India ($j \in TAGS$)

θ^{K}_{j1} : Capital's share of expenditure on primary inputs in industry j in India ($j \in TAGS^{C}$)

θ^{K}_{j3} : Capital's share of expenditure on second-stage aggregate of primary inputs in sector j in India ($j \in TAGS$)

θ^{F}_{j3} : Land's share of expenditure on second-stage aggregate of primary inputs in sector j in India ($j \in TAGS$)

θ^{VK}_{j} : Variable Capital's share of total cost in industry j in India ($j \in ALS$)

ρ_j : $1/(1-\sigma_j)$ ($j \in TRS$)

ρ^1_j : $1/(1-\overline{\sigma}_{j1})$ ($j \in TAGS^{C}$)

ρ^2_j : $1/(1-\overline{\sigma}_{j2})$ ($j \in TAGS$)

ρ^3_j : $1/(1-\overline{\sigma}_{j3})$ ($j \in TAGS$)

σ_j : Elasticity of substitution between imported and varieties of good j produced by representative firms/industry in India ($j \in TRS$)

$\overline{\sigma}_{j1}$: Elasticity of substitution between capital and labor in industry j in India ($j \in TAGS^{C}$)

$\overline{\sigma}_{j2}$: Elasticity of substitution between labor and composite of capital and land in sector j in India ($j \in TAGS$)

$\overline{\sigma}_{j3}$: Elasticity of substitution between capital and land in sector j in India ($j \in TAGS$)

η^{R}_{j} : Demand elasticity of India's export of good j ($j \in TRS$)

TABLE A.1. Sectoral Sets Specification

ALS	all sectors (1⋯34)
TRS	tradable sectors (1...34 except rail transport, i.e. 31)
NTS	non-traded sectors (31 only)
TPCS	tradable perfect competition sectors (1...4, 29...34 except 31)
TAGS	agricultural sectors (1...4)
TNAGS	tradable non-agriculture perfect competition sectors (29...34 ex-

	cept 31)
TAGSAP	TAGS under administered price (1,2)
TAGSNA	TAGS under free price (3, 4)
TSMS	tradable state monopoly sectors (16, 20, 27, 28)
TICS	tradable imperfect competition sectors (5...27 except TSMS)
TICSAP	TICS under administered price (12, 14, 21)
TMCS	TICS under monopolistic competition (TICS except TICSAP)
NSMS	non-traded state monopoly sectors (31)
SMS	state monopoly sectors (TSMS and NSMS)
APS	sectors under administered prices (TAGSAP, TSMS, TICSAP, NSMS)

Relationships among the sets:

ALS = TRS + NTS
TRS = TICS + TSMS + TPCS
TPCS = TAGS + TNAGS
TAGS = TAGSAP + TAGSNA
TICS = TMCS + TICSAP
NTS = NSMS
SMS = TSMS + NSMS
APS = TAGSAP + SMS + TICSAP
TAPS = APS – NSMS

For any set of sectors S, S^c is the complement of S, that is, all sectors in ALS that are *not* in S.

TABLE A.2. Mapping of Sets of Sectors

INDIA MODEL SECTOR	ISIC SECTOR	SETS ALS	TRS	NTS	TPCS
1. Paddy (PAD)	1A	X	X		X
2. Wheat (WHT)	1B	X	X		X
3. Other cereals (OCR)	1C	X	X		X
4. Rest of agriculture (ROA)	1D	X	X		X
5. Food, bev. & tobacco (FBT)	310	X	X		
6. Textiles (TEX)	321	X	X		
7. Clothing (CLO)	322	X	X		
8. Leather products (LPR)	323	X	X		
9. Footwear (FWR)	324	X	X		
10. Wood products (WPR)	331	X	X		
11. Furniture fixtures (FRF)	332	X	X		
12. Paper products (PPR)	341	X	X		
13. Printing & publishing (PRP)	342	X	X		
14. Fertilizer (FRT)	35A	X	X		
15. Other chemicals (OCH)	35B	X	X		
16. Petroleum products (PET)	35C	X	X		
17. Rubber products (RPR)	355	X	X		
18. Non-met. min. prod. (NMM)	36A	X	X		
19. Glass products (GPR)	362	X	X		
20. Iron & steel (IRS)	371	X	X		
21. Non-ferrous metal (NFM)	372	X	X		
22. Metal products (MPR)	381	X	X		
23. Non-elec. machinery (NEM)	382	X	X		
24. Electrical machinery (ELM)	383	X	X		
25. Transport equipment (TRE)	384	X	X		
26. Misc. manufacturing (MMF)	38A	X	X		
27. Mining & quarrying (MNQ)	2	X	X		
28. Elec., gas & water (EGW)	4	X	X		
29. Construction (CON)	5	X	X		X
30. Whole. & ret. trade (WRT)	6	X	X		X
31. Rail transport (RLT)	7A	X		X	
32. Oth. tran., st. & com. (TSC)	7B	X	X		X
33. Fin., ins. & real est. (FIR)	8	X	X		X
34. Com., so. & per. serv. (CSP)	9	X	X		X

INDIA MODEL SECTOR	ISIC SECTOR	TAGS	SETS		
			TNAGS	TAGSAP	SETS
1. Paddy (PAD)	1A	X		X	
2. Wheat (WHT)	1B	X		X	
3. Other cereals (OCR)	1C	X			X
4. Rest of agriculture (ROA)	1D	X			X
5. Food, bev. & tobacco (FBT)	310				
6. Textiles (TEX)	321				
7. Clothing (CLO)	322				
8. Leather products (LPR)	323				
9. Footwear (FWR)	324				
10. Wood products (WPR)	331				
11. Furniture fixtures (FRF)	332				
12. Paper products (PPR)	341				
13. Printing & publishing (PRP)	342				
14. Fertilizer (FRT)	35A				
15. Other chemicals (OCH)	35B				
16. Petroleum products (PET)	35C				
17. Rubber products (RPR)	355				
18. Non-met. min. prod. (NMM)	36A				
19. Glass products (GPR)	362				
20. Iron & steel (IRS)	371				
21. Non-ferrous metal (NFM)	372				
22. Metal products (MPR)	381				
23. Non-elec. machinery (NEM)	382				
24. Electrical machinery (ELM)	383				
25. Transport equipment (TRE)	384				
26. Misc. manufacturing (MMF)	38A				
27. Mining & quarrying (MNQ)	2				
28. Elec., gas & water (EGW)	4				
29. Construction (CON)	5		X		
30. Whole. & ret. trade (WRT)	6		X		
31. Rail transport (RLT)	7A				
32. Oth. tran., st. & com. (TSC)	7B		X		
33. Fin., ins. & real est. (FIR)	8		X		
34. Com., so. & per. serv. (CSP)	9		X		

(continued)

Table A.2. *(Continued)*

INDIA MODEL SECTOR	ISIC SECTOR	TSMS	SETS TICS	TICSAP	TMCS
1. Paddy (PAD)	1A				
2. Wheat (WHT)	1B				
3. Other cereals (OCR)	1C				
4. Rest of agriculture (ROA)	1D				
5. Food, bev. & tobacco (FBT)	310		X		X
6. Textiles (TEX)	321		X		X
7. Clothing (CLO)	322		X		X
8. Leather products (LPR)	323		X		X
9. Footwear (FWR)	324		X		X
10. Wood products (WPR)	331		X		X
11. Furniture fixtures (FRF)	332		X		X
12. Paper products (PPR)	341		X	X	
13. Printing & publishing (PRP)	342		X		X
14. Fertilizer (FRT)	35A		X	X	
15. Other chemicals (OCH)	35B		X		X
16. Petroleum products (PET)	35C	X			
17. Rubber products (RPR)	355		X		X
18. Non-met. min. prod. (NMM)	36A		X		X
19. Glass products (GPR)	362		X		X
20. Iron & steel (IRS)	371	X			
21. Non-ferrous metal (NFM)	372		X	X	
22. Metal products (MPR)	381		X		X
23. Non-elec. machinery (NEM)	382		X		X
24. Electrical machinery (ELM)	383		X		X
25. Transport equipment (TRE)	384		X		X
26. Misc. manufacturing (MMF)	38A		X		X
27. Mining & quarrying (MNQ)	2	X			
28. Elec., gas & water (EGW)	4	X			
29. Construction (CON)	5				
30. Whole. & ret. trade (WRT)	6				
31. Rail transport (RLT)	7A				
32. Oth. tran., st. & com. (TSC)	7B				
33. Fin., ins. & real est. (FIR)	8				
34. Com., so. & per. serv. (CSP)	9				

INDIA MODEL SECTOR	ISIC	SETS			
	SECTOR	NSMS	SMS	APS	TAPS
1. Paddy (PAD)	1A			X	X
2. Wheat (WHT)	1B			X	X
3. Other cereals (OCR)	1C				
4. Rest of agriculture (ROA)	1D				
5. Food, bev. & tobacco (FBT)	310				
6. Textiles (TEX)	321				
7. Clothing (CLO)	322				
8. Leather products (LPR)	323				
9. Footwear (FWR)	324				
10. Wood products (WPR)	331				
11. Furniture fixtures (FRF)	332				
12. Paper products (PPR)	341			X	X
13. Printing & publishing (PRP)	342				
14. Fertilizer (FRT)	35A			X	X
15. Other chemicals (OCH)	35B				
16. Petroleum products (PET)	35C		X	X	X
17. Rubber products (RPR)	355				
18. Non-met. min. prod. (NMM)	36A				
19. Glass products (GPR)	362				
20. Iron & steel (IRS)	371		X	X	X
21. Non-ferrous metal (NFM)	372			X	X
22. Metal products (MPR)	381				
23. Non-elec. machinery (NEM)	382				
24. Electrical machinery (ELM)	383				
25. Transport equipment (TRE)	384				
26. Misc. manufacturing (MMF)	38A				
27. Mining & quarrying (MNQ)	2		X	X	X
28. Elec., gas & water (EGW)	4		X	X	X
29. Construction (CON)	5				
30. Whole. & ret. trade (WRT)	6				
31. Rail transport (RLT)	7A	X	X	X	
32. Oth. tran., st. & com. (TSC)	7B				
33. Fin., ins. & real est. (FIR)	8				
34. Com., so. & per. serv. (CSP)	9				

Notes to Appendix 1

[1] The notation representing sets of sectors (*ALS*, etc.) is explained in Tables A.1 and A.2. The list of variables and parameters is given below. In the text, we follow the convention that a hat (^) over a variable indicates the change in the logarithm of the variable, or approximately its per cent change. Also, Δ before a variable indicates the absolute change (as opposed to change in logarithm) in the variable.

[2] See Chadha, Djankov, and Pohit (1995) for derivational notes.

Appendix 2

DATA BASE AND PARAMETERS

List of Tables

List of Variables/Parameters

Variable/ Parameter Notation	Variable/Parameter Name	Table
b_{j0}	Primary input share of total cost in industry j in India	18
bt_j	Other tax (net of subsidies) share of total industry j in India	18
D^I_{j0}	Domestic demand for sector j	11
D^I_{jF}	Final demand for sector j	11
D^I_j	Demand in India for jth good produced by a representative firm in India	12
D^M_j	Imported demand for good j produced by ROW	12
D^R_j	Demand for jth good produced by a representative firm/industry in India	12
E_j	Aggregate expenditure on good j	12
η_j	Perceived elasticity of demand by a firm in sector j in India	21
η^M_j	Demand elasticity for India's Import of good j	7
η^R_j	Demand elasticity for India's Export of good j	6
F^0	Total land stock	9
h^F_j	Fraction of land in India allocated to sector j	9
$h^F_j F^0_j$	Land allocated to agricultural sector	9
h^K_j	Fraction of capital employed in sector j	10
$h^K_j K^0_j$	Capital employed in sector j	10
h^L_j	Fraction of labor employed in sector j	11
$h^L_j L^0_j$	Labor force employed in sector j	11
b_{ij}	Input-output coefficients	17
K^0	Total capital stock	9
L^0	Total labor force	9
n_j	Number of firms in sector j	10
NT_j	Net production tax in sector j	14
S_j	Production of good j	11
σ_j	Elasticity of substitution among varieties of good j	8

σ_{j2}, σ_{j3}	Elasticity of substitution between factors of production	8
$\overline{\sigma}_{j1}$	Elasticity of substitution between capital and labor	8
t_j	Tariff imposed by India on Imports of good j	14
θ^F_{j3}	Land's share of expenditure on 2nd stage aggregate of primary inputs in sector j	22
θ^{FC}_j	Fixed input share of total cost in sector j	23
θ^K_{j1}	Capital's share of expenditure on primary inputs in sector j	22
θ^K_{j3}	Capital's share of expenditure on second stage of primary inputs in sector j	22
θ^{KF}_{j2}	Share of composite land/capital expenditure on 1st stage aggregate of primary input	22
θ_j	Fraction of expenditure in India on home good j	16
θ^L_{j1}	Labor's share of expenditure on primary inputs in sector j	22
θ^L_{j2}	Labor's share of expenditure on first stage aggregate of primary inputs in sector j	22
θ^M_j	Fraction of expenditure in India on imported good j	16
θ^{MC}_j	Variable input share of total cost in sector j	23
θ^{MQ}_j	Fraction of imports of goods j by India that are subject to quantitative restriction	15
θ^{VK}_j	Variable capital's share of total capital employed in sector j	23
θ^{XQ}_j	Fraction of exports of good j by India subject to quantitative restriction	15
t^X_j	Export tax imposed by India on its export of good j	14
$vd_{i,j}$	Intermediate demand for good j by industry i's share of total purchases of good j in India	20
v_{j0}	Final demand share of total purchases of good j in India	19

LIST OF VARIABLES / COEFFICIENTS

Variable / Coefficient Notation	Variable / Coefficient Name	Page
b0 (j)	Primary input share of total cost in indusutry j in India	110
bt (j)	Other tax net of subsidies share of total cost in industry j in India	110
demand_dm (j)	Domestic demand for sector j	101
demand_fm (j)	Final demand for sector j	101
Di (j)	Demand of jth good produced by a representative firm in India by India	102
Di (j) / n (j)	Demand of jth good produced by a representative firm in India by India	102
Dm (j)	Imported demand of good j produced by ROW	102
Dr (j)	Demand of jth good produced by a representative firm/industry in India by ROW	102
E (j)	Aggregate expenditure on good j	102
eta (j)	Percieved elasticity of demand by a firm in sector j in India	116
etam (j)	Demand elasticity of India's Import of good j	95
etar (j)	Demand elasticity of India's Export of good j	94
Fo	Total Land stock	97
hF (j)	Fraction of land in India allocated to sector j	97
hF (j) * F0 (j)	Land allocated to agricultural sector	97
hK (j)	Fraction of Capital employed in sector j	98
hK (j) * K0 (j)	Capital employed in sector j	98
hL (j)	Fraction of Labour employed in sector j	99
hL (j) * L0 (j)	Labour force employed in sector j	99
Input-Output Transaction Table		89-93
iom (i,j)	Input - Output Coefficients	106-109
Ko	Total Capital stock	98
Lo	Total Labour force	99
n (j)	Number of Firms in sector j	100
nt (j)	Net production Tax in sector j	103
S (j)	Production of good j	101
Sigma (j)	Elasticities of substitution between different varieties of good j	96
Sigma2 (j) / Sigma3 (j)	Elasticities of substitution between factors of production	96
Sigmabar1 (j)	Elasticities of substitution between capital and labour	96
t (j)	Tariff imposed by India on Imports of good j	103
thetaF3 (j)	Land's share of expenditure on 2nd stage aggregate of primary inputs in sector j	118
thetaFC (j)	Fixed input share of total cost in sector j	119
thetaK1 (j)	Capital's share of expenditure on primary inputs in sector j	117
thetaK3 (j)	Capital's share of expenditure on second stage of primary inputs in sector j	118
thetaKF2 (j)	Share of composite land/capital expenditure on 1st stage aggregate of primary input	118
thetal (j)	Fraction of expenditure in India on home good j	105
thetaL1 (j)	Labour's share of expenditure on primary inputs in sector j	117

LIST OF VARIABLES / COEFFICIENTS

Variable / Coefficient Notation	Variable / Coefficient Name	Page
thetaL2 (j)	Labour's share of expenditure on first stage aggregate of primary inputs in sector j	118
thetaM (j)	Fraction of expenditure in India on imported good j	105
thetaMC (j)	Variable input share of total cost in sector j	119
thetaMQ (j)	Fraction of Import of goods j by India that are subjected to quantitative restriction	104
thetaVK (j)	Variable capital's share of total capital employed in sector j	119
thetaXQ (j)	Fraction of Export of goods j by India subjected to quantitative restriction	104
tx (j)	Export tax imposed by India on its export of good j	103
vd (i,j)	Intermediate demand for good j by industry j's share of total purchases of good j in India	112-115
vo (j)	Final demand share of total purchases of good j in India	111

Table 1. Mapping for Concordance between India Model Sectors & 60 (115) Sectors of Input – Output Table

Sectors of India Model	ISIC Code	Input-Output (60 x 60) sectors	Input-Output (115 x 115) sectors	Method used in calculating proportionate weightage for Selected groups based on 1983-84 (115 x 115) Input Output matrix
1 Paddy	1A	1	001	
2 Wheet	1B	2	002	
3 Other Cereals	1C	3	003+004+005	
4 Other Agriculture	1D	4 to 14	006 to 022	
5 Food, Beverages, Tobacco	310	20 to 23	33 to 40	
6 Textiles	321	24 to 28 less (48)	41 to 47,49	
7 Clothing	322	(48)	48	Clothing / (Textiles + clothing)
8 Leather products	323	31 less (54)	55	
9 Footwear	324	(54)	54	Footwear / (Leather products + footwear)
10 Wood & Wood products	331	29 less (50)	51	
11 Furnitures & Fixtures	332	(50)	50	Furniture & Fixtures / (Wood & Wood products + Furniture & Fixtures)
12 Paper Products	341	30 less (53)	52	
13 Printing & publishing	342	(53)	53	Printing & Publishing / (Paper products + Printing & Publishing)
14 Fertilizers	35A	36	62	
15 Other Chemicals	35B	35 + 37 + 38 + 39	59 to 61,63 to 68	
16 Petroleum Products	35C	34	58	
17 Rubber Products	355	32	56	
18 Non-metallic mineral products	36A	40 + 41 less (71)	69 + 70	
19 Glass Products	362	(71)	71	Glass Products / (Non-metallic Products + Glass Products)
20 Iron & steel	371	42	72+73+74	
21 Non-ferrous metals	372	43	75	
22 Metal products	381	(76 + 77)	76+77	
23 Non-electrical Machinery & parts	382	44 + 45 + 46	78 to 83	
24 Electrical machinery	383	47 + 48 + 49	84 to 90	
25 Transport equipment & parts	384	50 + 51 + 52	91 to 96	
26 Other misc. manufacturing industries	38A	53 + 33 less (76 + 77)	57 + 97 + 98	Misc.Manufacturing / (Misc.Manufacturing + Metal Products)
27 Mining,Quarying	2	15 to 19	23 to 32	
28 Electricity,Gas&Water Supply	4	55	100 to 102	
29 Construction	5	54	99	
30 Wholesale&Retail Trade	6	59	107	
31 Rail Transport	7A	56	103	
32 Transport, Storage & Communication	7B	57 + (106) + (105)	104 +105 +106	Transport, Storage & Communication / (104+105+106+109+110+111+108+112+113+114+115)
33 Finance, Insurance & Real Estate	8	58	109 +110 +111	Finance, Insurance & Estates / (104+105+106+109+110+111+112+113+114+115)

34	Community, Social & Personnel Services	9	60 less (106 – 105) less 108 +112 +113 +114 +115 (109 + 110 + 111) + Community, Social & Personnel Services / (104+105+106+108+109+110+111+112+113+114+115)

Note: Figures in bracket represent the code numbers of 115 x 115 matrix

Table 2. Mapping for Concordance between India Model Sectors & National Industrial Classification, version 1970

Sectors of India Model	ISIC Code	3 digit code of National Industrial Classification 1970
5 Food, Beverages, Tobacco	310	200 to 229
6 Textiles	321	230+233+234+235+236+231+232+240+241+242+243+245+246+247+248+250+253+ 251+252+260+261+263+262+244+268+259+266+267+269
7 Clothing	322	264+(265 less 265.1)+292+295
8 Leather products	323	290+294+293+299+296
9 Footwear	324	291
10 Wood & Wood products	331	271+270+272+273+274+275+279
11 Furnitures & Fixtures	332	276+277
12 Paper Products	341	280+281+282+283
13 Printing & publishing	342	284+285+286+287+288+289
14 Fertilizers	35A	311
15 Other Chemicals	35B	310+313+314+315+316+317+318+319
16 Petroleum Products	35C	304+305+306+307
17 Rubber Products	355	300+301+302
18 Non-metallic mineral products	36A	322+327+323+320+324+325+326+328+329
19 Glass Products	362	321 less 321.5
20 Iron & steel	371	330+331+332
21 Non-ferrous metals	372	333+334+335+336+339
22 Metal products	381	352+351+350+353+354+355+356+357+358+359+366
23 Non-electrical Machinery & parts	382	340+341+342+343+344+345+349
24 Electrical machinery	383	360+364+363+361+362+365+369+367
25 Transport equipment & parts	384	370+371+372+373+374+375+376+377+378+379
26 Other misc. manufacturing industries	38A	380+366.2+381+382+383+384+385+386+387+389+303+312+265.1+321.5
27 Mining,Quarying	2	100 to 199
28 Electricity,Gas & Water Supply	4	400+410+401+420
29 Construction	5	500 to 519
30 Wholesale & Retail Trade	6	600 to 691
31 Rail Transport	7A	700
32 Transport, Storage & Communication	7B	701 to 759
33 Finance, Insurance & Real Estate	8	800 to 899
34 Community, Social & Personnel Services	9	900 to 990

Note: The Mapping excludes the four agricultural sectors (i.e. Codes 1A to 1D)

Table 3. Mapping for Concordance between India Model Sectors & National Industrial Classification, version 1987

	Sectors of India Model	ISIC Code	3 digit codes of National Industrial Classification 1987
5	Food, Beverages, Tobacco	310	200 to 229
6	Textiles	321	230+231+232+233+234+235+236+240+241+242+243+244+245+246+247+248+250 251+252+253+254+255+256+257+258+259+260+261+262+263+264+267+268+269
7	Clothing	322	265+266+292+295
8	Leather products	323	290+294+293+299+296
9	Footwear	324	291
10	Wood & Wood products	331	270+271+272+273+274+275+279
11	Furnitures & Fixtures	332	276+277
12	Paper Products	341	280+281+282+283
13	Printing & publishing	342	284+285+286+287+288+289
14	Fertilizers	35A	301
15	Other Chemicals	35B	300+302+306+304+305+307+308+309+317
16	Petroleum Products	35C	314+315+316+318+319
17	Rubber Products	355	310+311+312
18	Non-metallic mineral products	36A	322+323+320+324+325+326+327+329
19	Glass Products	362	321
20	Iron & steel	371	330+331+332
21	Non-ferrous metals	372	333+334+335+336+337+338+339
22	Metal products	381	343+346+342+340+341+344+345+349
23	Non-electrical Machinery & parts	382	352+391+350+390+357+392+351+353+354+393+358+355+356+359+399
24	Electrical machinery	383	360+395+365+366+368+396+364+361+362+363+369+367+394
25	Transport equipment & parts	384	370+371+372+397+373+374+398+375+376+377+378+379
26	Other misc. manufacturing industries	38A	380+381+382+383+384+386+385+387+388+389+313+303
27	Mining,Quarying	2	100 to 199
28	Electricity,Gas & Water Supply	4	400+401+410+420
29	Construction	5	500 to 519
30	Wholesale & Retail Trade	6	600 to 691
31	Rail Transport	7A	700
32	Transport, Storage & Communication	7B	701 to 759
33	Finance, Insurance & Real Estate	8	800 to 899
34	Community, Social & Personnel Services	9	900 to 990

Note: The Mapping excludes the four agricultural sectors (i.e. Codes 1A to 1D)

Table 4. Mapping for Concordance between India Model Sectors & 6 Digits Codes of Indian Trade Classification System (Harmonized Series)

1A	1B	1C	1D	310
100600-100640	100100-100190	70800-70890+	30600-30629+	20100-21090+
		100200-100590+	30731-30731+	30729-30729+
		100700-100890	30751-30751+	30749-30749+
			30791-30791+	30799-30799+
			40900-40900+	40800-40899+
			60100-60499+	50400-50790+
			71400-71490+	30500-30569+
			120900-121490+	30739-30739+
			140100-140490+	30759-30759+
			180100-180100+	40100-40690+
			310100-310100+	51100-51199+
			410100-410390+	41000-41000+
			440100-440420+	71000-71290+
			500100-500200+	80100-80290+
			520100-520100+	90100-91099+
			530200-530210+	110100-110630+
			530400-530410+	120800-120890+
			530521-530521+	150100-150430+
			710100-710110+	160100-160590+
			30100-30490+	180200-180690+
			30700-30721+	200100-200990+
			30741-30741+	220900-220900+
			30760-30760+	230400-230690+
			40700-40700+	250100-250100+
			50800-51000+	350200-350290+
			70100-70990+	71300-71390+
			80300-81090+	81100-81400+
			120100-120799+	100620-100640+
			130100-130190+	110800-110900+
			170100-170112+	130220-130220+
			240100-240130+	150600-151800+
			400110-400130+	170191-170490+
			430100 430190+	190100-190590+
			450100-450190+	210100-210690+
			510100-510220+	230100-210320+
			530100-530129+	230800-230990+
			530300-530310+	350100-350110+
			530500-530511+	110700-110720+
			530591-530591	220300-220300+
				220700-220890+
				230700-230700+
				220100-220290+
				220400-220600+
				230330-230330+
				240200-240399

321	322	323	324	331
150500-150590+	420300-420340+	410400-411100+	640200-640620+	440500-441300+
500300-500790+	620100-621790+	420400-420690+	640699-640699	441500-441600+
520200-521225+	650100-650700+	430400-430400+		441800-441890+
530290-530290+	430300-430390+	420100-420299+		450200-450490+
530490-530490+	630900-630900	430200-430230		441400-441400+
530529-530529+				441700-441700+
530600-531100+				441900-442190+
540600-540834+				460200-460290+
560100-560300+				640691-640691
560500-560600+				
560900-560990+				
460100-460199+				
510300-511300+				
530130-530130+				
530390-530390+				
530519-530519+				
530599-530599+				
540100-540349+				
550500-551694+				
560420-560490+				
560700-560890+				
570100-570500+				
580100-580900+				
590100-590500+				
600100-600299+				
630100-630190+				
630221-630239+				
630251-630299+				
630391-630399+				
630419-630419+				
630492-630499+				
630800-630800+				
701900-701920+				
581000-581100+				
590700-591190+				
610100-611790+				
630200-630210+				
630240-630240+				
630300-630319+				
630400-630411+				
630491-630491+				
630500-630790+				
631000-631090				

Table 4. *(Continued)*

332	341	342	35A	35B
940150-40169+	380300-380300+	481720-481720+	310200-310290+	151900-151930+
940380-40390+	480100-480640+	482100-482110+	310300-310590	270700-270799+
940600-40600+	480791-480799+	490100-491199+		280100-280200+
940330-40360+	481000-481500+	482000-482090+		290100-293500+
940400-940490	481730-481730+	482340-482351		294200-294200+
	481900-481960+			262100-262100+
	482200-482290+			271100-271119+
	482320-482320+			280400-285100+
	482359-482390+			294000-294000+
	470100-470790+			320100-320740+
	480700-480710+			350710-350790+
	480800-480890+			380500-380590+
				380630+380700+
	481700-481710+			390100-391400+
	481800-481890+			400200-400299+
	482190-482190+			550100-550490+
	482300-482319+			340391-340399+
	482330-482330			380100-380290+
				380610-380620+
				380690-380690+
				380800-380830+
				391500-391690+
				540400-540500+
				130200-130211+
				130231-130231+
				152000-152090+
				280300-280300+
				294100-294190+
				300620-300630+
				320800-321290+
				321500-321590+
				330300-330790+
				340100-340190+
				340540-340540+
				340600-340600+
				350300-350699+
				370100-370790+
				380840-380890+
				381400-381400+
				381700-382000+
				382200-382390+
				130212-130219+
				130232-130239+
				152100-152200+
				293600-293990+
				300100-300490+
				300660-300660+
				321400-321490+
				330100-330290+
				340111-340290+
				340500-340530+
				340590-340590+
				350190-350190+
				360100-360690+
				380400-380400

35C	355	36A	362	371
271000-271000+	401100-401390+	690900-691490+	700100-701890+	261800-261900+
271200-271390+	401400-401700+	854700-854710+	854600-854610+	731500-731600+
271121-271129+	590600-590699+	854620-854620+	702000-702000	720100-722990
270120-270120+	400300-401099+	252020-252020+		
270600-270600+	560400-560410+	381600-381600+		
271500-271500+	640100-640199	252200-252390+		
680700-680790+		680100-680690+		
270400-270400+		680800-681599+		
270800-270820+		690300-690390+		
340311-340319		701931-701990+		
		690100-690290+		
		690400-690890+		
		732300-732310		

(continued)

Table 4. *(Continued)*

372	381	382	383	384
262000-262090+	730100-730799+	830700-830790+	842430-842430+	850100-850590+
711500-711590+	731000-731450+	840100-840140+	842489-842490+	850900-851090+
750100-750720+	732000-732290+	840619-840690+	842900-843069+	851300-851390+
780100-780500+	732400-732690+	840820-840890+	843141-843149+	851600-851690+
800100-800600+	750800-750800+	841000-841090+	843500-843590+	853200-853990+
710600-711100+	761200-761690+	841300-841590+	843700-844900+	854100-854290+
740100-741220+	790700-790790+	842000-842099+	845100-845190+	854690-854690+
760100-760900+	820100-821599+	842200-842219+	845300-845390+	854800-854800+
790100-790600+	830300-830300+	842300-842390	846900-847340+	850600-850790+
810100-811300	830500-830590+		847600-847690+	851100-851190+
	830621-830630+		847900-847990+	851400-851490+
	830900-831190+		850800-850890+	851700-853190+
	841600-841690+		930100-930700+	854000-854099+
	940110-940140+		830820-830890+	854300-854590+
	940300-940320+		840500-840590+	854790-854790+
	961700-961700+		840731-840790+	902200-902290
	730800-730900+		840991-840999+	
	731700-731829+		841200-841290+	
	732391-732399+		841700-841990+	
	741300-741999+		842100-842199+	
	761000-761100+		842220-842290+	
	780600-780600+		842420-842420+	
	800700-800700+		842481-842481+	
	830100-830260+		842500-842890+	
	830400-830400+		843100-843139+	
	830600-830610+		843200-843490+	
	830800-830810+		843600-843699+	
	840200-840490+		845000-845090+	
	842400-842410+		845200-845290+	
	940171-940190+		845400-846890+	
	940500-940599		847400-847590+	
			847700-847890+	
			848000 848590+	
			851500-851590	

38A	2
300500-300590+	250200-252010+
300640-300650+	252400-253090 +
901400-902190+	270111-270119+
910100-911490+	270900-270900+
300600-300610+	252100-252100+
900100-901390+	260100-261790+
902300-903300+	270200-270300+
940200-940290+	271400-271490
50100-50300+	
271600-271600+	
340700-340700+	
481600-481690+	
670100-670490+	
710200-710590+	
711300-711420+	
731900-731990+	
920100-920999+	
950600-950790+	
960100-961620+	
970100-970600+	
270500-270500+	
321300-321390+	
480900-480990+	
660100-660390+	
710121-710122+	
711200-711290+	
711600-711890+	
860900-860900+	
950100-950590+	
950800-950800+	
961800-961800+	
391700-392690+	
940370-940370+	
854720-854720+	

Note: The Indian Trade Classification System only covers India Model sectors of ISIC codes 1A to 2.

Table 5. Input-Output Transactions, year 1989-90 (unit : Rs. million)

SN SECTOR	ISIC Code	1	2	3	4	5	6	7	8	9
1. Paddy	1A	33881	39	0	6764	1469	20	62	0	0
2. Wheat	1B	119	19947	0	7935	3679	28	1	0	0
3. Other Cereals	1C	19	12	1011	5680	842	1	0	0	0
4. Rest of Agriculture	1D	24009	9314	9444	241743	134979	69962	4	4807	430
5. Food, Beverage and Tobacco	310	71	12	0	12103	42456	500	1	189	0
6. Textiles	321	432	107	0	4033	3779	128241	17756	246	738
7. Clothing	322	1	1	0	36	1	57	3265	0	0
8. Leather Products	323	0	0	0	0	1	76	2	2448	3920
9. Footwear	324	0	0	0	0	0	0	0	0	17
10. Wood Products	331	3	1	0	13	493	1133	23	60	25
11. Furniture Fixtures	332	0	0	0	11	0	0	0	0	10
12. Paper Products	341	24	14	1	168	2629	3016	358	36	213
13. Printing and Publishing	342	11	7	1	69	5	129	0	0	0
14. Fertilizer	35A	16691	10475	2712	34149	48	4	0	0	0
15. Other Chemicals	35B	1147	358	28	8776	5584	25368	74	1159	377
16. Petroleum Products	35C	4269	2193	999	9797	3607	6474	374	99	65
17. Rubber Products	355	5	4	0	114	1	47	23	21	1877
18. Non-metallic Mineral Products	36A	1	0	0	1	0	0	0	0	0
19. Glass Products	362	0	0	0	4	797	6	0	29	0
20. Iron and Steel	371	0	0	0	22	241	394	0	10	2
21. Non-ferrous Metal	372	0	0	0	3	146	732	0	16	0
22. Metal Products	381	150	40	0	674	5647	2717	799	105	134
23. Non-electrical Machinery	382	1667	1063	637	3880	1100	2380	364	33	37
24. Electrical Machinery	383	8	6	1	56	1	3	0	1	0
25. Transport Equipment	384	251	182	198	1649	2	3	0	2	0
26. Miscellaneous Manufacturing	38A	27	13	0	319	1520	1192	2021	43	141
27. Mining and Quarrying	2	148	299	0	303	2702	3357	359	28	40
28. Electricity, Gas and Water	4	2607	5121	228	5354	3655	26825	1613	169	158
29. Construction	5	7782	3944	3114	19267	2101	1467	670	108	86
30. Wholesale and Retail Trade	6	7007	3512	777	39894	28648	35371	3615	1731	2114
31. Rail Transport	7A	1540	1099	207	3606	1334	1449	130	35	22
32. Other Transport, Storage and Communication	7B	2793	1436	395	11705	8870	16776	0	1054	0
33. Finance, Insurance, and Real Estate	8	2330	964	660	7719	6183	11127	0	1297	0
34. Commercial, Social and Personal Services	9	912	254	3	2948	11068	27593	0	1141	0
Total		107907	60416	20414	428794	273590	366448	31512	14868	10409
Indirect Tax Less Subsidies		-11178	-8194	-1261	-15074	13149	21676	1197	549	821
Gross Value Added		208544	101573	56845	861022	61191	131840	56155	2500	7055
Gross Output		305273	153795	75998	1274742	347930	519963	88864	17917	18285

SN SECTOR	ISIC Code	10	11	12	13	14	15	16	17	18
1. Paddy	1A	1	0	1	0	4	2204	1	0	53
2. Wheat	1B	0	0	4	0	0	82	0	0	18
3. Other Cereals	1C	0	0	0	0	0	12	0	0	0
4. Rest of Agriculture	1D	13971	398	2151	6	33	6552	88	4250	568
5. Food, Beverage and Tobacco	310	3	0	131	2	18	4968	17	4	21
6. Textiles	321	27	58	579	290	1931	3985	152	2488	2455
7. Clothing	322	0	0	109	0	0	1	0	0	0
8. Leather Products	323	5	2	0	11	0	3	0	168	0
9. Footwear	324	0	0	0	0	0	0	0	0	0
10. Wood Products	331	271	502	32	23	10	611	40	29	15
11. Furniture Fixtures	332	3	301	0	0	0	0	0	0	0
12. Paper Products	341	5	20	13849	15612	87	7299	179	198	62
13. Printing and Publishing	342	1	0	137	233	0	15	0	0	0
14. Fertilizer	35A	0	0	0	0	6675	100	0	0	0
15. Other Chemicals	35B	106	24	2332	1029	8175	55949	3311	6802	258
16. Petroleum Products	35C	72	8	742	163	8342	8203	16717	499	2472
17. Rubber Products	355	6	4	1	19	0	100	0	4877	52
18. Non-metallic Mineral Products	36A	0	0	0	11	0	24	1	0	391
19. Glass Products	362	7	0	0	35	11	1194	0	71	272
20. Iron and Steel	371	38	19	49	79	3	247	1	234	706
21. Non-ferrous Metal	372	9	7	1374	0	32	2476	7	71	518
22. Metal Products	381	61	45	564	337	474	7427	1626	734	732
23. Non-electrical Machinery	382	54	0	198	254	215	817	57	66	341
24. Electrical Machinery	383	3	0	7	0	0	8	0	5	0
25. Transport Equipment	384	6	0	6	0	0	4	0	67	1
26. Miscellaneous Manufacturing	38A	39	79	129	372	370	2490	274	154	131
27. Mining and Quarrying	2	33	6	2372	27	6281	13383	82651	292	12365
28. Electricity, Gas and Water	4	210	19	2809	760	5542	9935	934	442	3096
29. Construction	5	115	2	181	94	262	1009	278	273	526
30. Wholesale and Retail Trade	6	1816	153	2411	1581	5211	17457	7685	4144	4876
31. Rail Transport	7A	114	7	639	102	1098	3476	708	86	1820
32. Other Transport, Storage and Communication	7B	643	102	1827	0	1529	7317	1638	1072	2682
33. Finance, Insurance, and Real Estate	8	27	5	3479	0	2647	6822	3507	1055	1642
34. Commercial, Social and Personal Services	9	301	329	2545	0	1300	7957	383	910	4663
Total		17948	2091	38659	21041	50253	172127	120254	28992	40736
Indirect Tax Less Subsidies		717	76	2237	1887	775	23627	44306	4638	2727
Gross Value Added		5617	1303	8315	13783	11266	57697	8821	12112	15454
Gross Output		24281	3470	49211	36711	62294	253451	173382	45742	58917

(continued)

Table 5. *(Continued)*

SN SECTOR	ISIC Code	28	29	30	31	32	33	34	TIU
1. Paddy	1A	1	0	49	0	59	0	8460	53076
2. Wheat	1B	2	0	23	0	112	0	5418	37373
3. Other Cereals	1C	0	0	5	0	25	0	0	7608
4. Rest of Agriculture	1D	306	18213	960	13	738	0	31695	576618
5. Food, Beverage and Tobacco	310	7	0	243	0	665	0	7637	69101
6. Textiles	321	0	1118	1733	73	366	2	10424	182731
7. Clothing	322	77	29	0	9	56	9	5793	9465
8. Leather Products	323	0	0	32	0	0	0	251	7033
9. Footwear	324	0	0	0	0	20	0	0	37
10. Wood Products	331	260	15285	1310	45	2	0	19	21799
11. Furniture Fixtures	332	8	21	0	14	2	2	1322	1747
12. Paper Products	341	193	304	2069	184	786	294	2367	54547
13. Printing and Publishing	342	116	638	1544	60	1623	450	13213	18442
14. Fertilizer	35A	1	524	54	0	0	0	313	71768
15. Other Chemicals	35B	320	19487	643	13	168	0	28215	193639
16. Petroleum Products	35C	3529	571	560	4473	36561	157	601	130507
17. Rubber Products	355	21	214	95	4	6562	22	18	19509
18. Non-metallic Mineral Products	36A	0	26484	35	0	0	0	4	29549
19. Glass Products	362	240	10033	0	187	23	0	473	18015
20. Iron and Steel	371	754	66590	1125	987	2591	0	254	192815
21. Non-ferrous Metal	372	49	0	294	0	0	0	1374	49949
22. Metal Products	381	449	298	2028	2078	715	4	1439	56645
23. Non-electrical Machinery	382	2343	846	274	208	1340	341	390	50002
24. Electrical Machinery	383	5279	20011	290	1762	3343	78	1164	66998
25. Transport Equipment	384	64	515	374	19593	16085	1252	167	66788
26. Miscellaneous Manufacturing	38A	2512	778	1680	70	1639	9	17143	53942
27. Mining and Quarrying	2	27711	30035	270	1967	304	0	3824	212841
28. Electricity, Gas and Water	4	53339	9736	5241	3307	4484	1536	5770	185000
29. Construction	5	4151	72	2325	7887	3549	27674	4693	101608
30. Wholesale and Retail Trade	6	7317	43602	8057	1384	9196	576	16328	293857
31. Rail Transport	7A	6882	8037	1818	802	2430	261	1356	50390
32. Other Transport, Storage and Communication	7B	3018	14260	52509	1091	23377	177	17443	187872
33. Finance, Insurance, and Real Estate	8	1398	6427	16870	3211	10825	562	21943	129234
34. Commercial, Social and Personal Services	9	1067	11491	26908	1872	8814	206	15804	168854
Total		121413	305619	129418	51295	136460	33613	225316	3369359
Indirect Tax Less Subsidies		5830	36164	3349	3272	25789	793	13491	261971
Gross Value Added		87928	220180	481920	46234	203671	371549	522509	3952116
Gross Output		215171	561963	614687	100801	365919	405956	761316	7583446

SN SECTOR	ISIC Code	PFCE	GFCE	GFCF	CIS	EXPORT	IMPORT	T_ OUTPUT
1. Paddy	1A	248374	299	0	2516	3836	2829	305273
2. Wheat	1B	111861	299	0	4457	19	214	153795
3. Other Cereals	1C	67795	0	0	811	19	235	75998
4. Rest of Agriculture	1D	648190	795	33260	3759	25118	12999	1274741
5. Food, Beverage and Tobacco	310	272102	196	0	678	10914	5061	347930
6. Textiles	321	281281	452	19823	15464	23770	3557	519963
7. Clothing	322	35476	290	0	1085	43206	659	88864
8. Leather Products	323	1089	1	0	10	10021	237	17917
9. Footwear	324	12812	0	0	216	5297	77	18285
10. Wood Products	331	1073	7	1614	0	138	351	24281
11. Furniture Fixtures	332	926	293	500	1	3	0	3471
12. Paper Products	341	2084	1789	0	311	158	9678	49211
13. Printing and Publishing	342	12655	6187	0	312	90	975	36711
14. Fertilizer	35A	0	612	0	2178	15	12279	62294
15. Other Chemicals	35B	64303	1606	0	21805	16029	43932	253450
16. Petroleum Products	35C	42137	9966	0	792	5303	15323	173382
17. Rubber Products	355	10096	467	9247	287	6765	629	45742
18. Non-metallic Mineral Products	36A	0	0	0	470	29076	178	58917
19. Glass Products	362	8865	1	243	199	23298	1534	49087
20. Iron and Steel	371	0	0	11999	705	2258	30619	177158
21. Non-ferrous Metal	372	0	0	0	538	906	14059	37334
22. Metal Products	381	7538	245	12226	1707	1093	12766	66688
23. Non-electrical Machinery	382	1094	3930	152408	5832	13033	90594	135705
24. Electrical Machinery	383	18050	952	94151	11967	10060	33494	168684
25. Transport Equipment	384	11995	2589	87457	7179	7213	21404	161818
26. Miscellaneous Manufacturing	38A	29406	21585	17492	6416	5338	14019	120160
27. Mining and Quarrying	2	2074	72	0	5895	4988	95098	130772
28. Electricity, Gas and Water	4	17141	12963	0	0	67	0	215171
29. Construction	5	0	46617	409409	0	8449	4119	561964
30. Wholesale and Retail Trade	6	233067	5565	35548	0	56046	9393	614688
31. Rail Transport	7A	37809	6566	6038	0	0	0	100802
32. Other Transport, Storage and Communication	7B	169313	10930	3901	0	42615	48712	365920
33. Finance, Insurance, and Real Estate	8	265148	8332	0	0	7042	3799	405957
34. Commercial, Social and Personal Services	9	218506	368286	0	0	5877	207	761316
Total		2832257	511892	895317	95590	368061	489030	7583446

(continued)

Table 5. *(Continued)*

SN	SECTOR	ISIC Code	PFCE	GFCE	GFCF	CIS	EXPORT	IMPORT	T_ OUTPUT
	Indirect Tax Less Subsidies		118532	18778	74103	0	2189	0	475573
	Gross Value Added		0	0	0	0	0	0	3952116
	Gross Output		2950790	530670	969420	95590	370250	489030	12011135

Note:
TIU: Total Intermediate Use
PFCE : Private Final Consumption Expenditure
GFCE : Government Final Consumption Expenditure
GFCF : Gross Fixed Investment
CIS : Changes in Stocks
T_OUTPUT : Total Output

Table 6. Elasticity (Exports)

SN SECTOR	ISIC Code	etar (j)	Source
1. Paddy	1A	-0.9200	Virmani (1991)
2. Wheat	1B	-0.9200	Virmani (1991)
3. Other Cereals	1C	-0.9200	Virmani (1991)
4. Rest of Agriculture	1D	-0.9200	Virmani (1991)
5. Food, Beverage and Tobacco	310	-1.1570	Lucas (1988)
6. Textiles	321	-3.3440	Lucas (1988)
7. Clothing	322	-1.6400	Virmani (1991)
8. Leather Products	323	-1.1070	Lucas (1988)
9. Footwear	324	-1.6400	Virmani (1991)
10. Wood Products	331	-1.0932	Pohit and Bhide (1994)
11. Furniture Fixtures	332	-1.0932	Pohit and Bhide (1994)
12. Paper Products	341	-1.0932	Pohit and Bhide (1994)
13. Printing and Publishing	342	-1.0932	Pohit and Bhide (1994)
14. Fertilizer	35A	-0.6940	Lucas (1988)
15. Other Chemicals	35B	-0.6940	Lucas (1988)
16. Petroleum Products	35C	-0.6940	Lucas (1988)
17. Rubber Products	355	-1.0650	Lucas (1988)
18. Non-metallic Mineral Products	36A	-1.0370	Lucas (1988)
19. Glass Products	362	-1.0370	Lucas (1988)
20. Iron and Steel	371	-2.5680	Lucas (1988)
21. Non-ferrous Metal	372	-5.4270	Lucas (1988)
22. Metal Products	381	-0.6840	Lucas (1988)
23. Non-electrical Machinery	382	-0.9790	Lucas (1988)
24. Electrical Machinery	383	-1.3760	Lucas (1988)
25. Transport Equipment	384	-1.6100	Lucas (1988)
26. Miscellaneous Manufacturing	38A	-1.6400	Ratha and Sahoo (1990)
27. Mining and Quarrying	2	-0.9200	Virmani (1991)
28. Electricity, Gas and Water	4	-1.0000	-
29. Construction	5	-1.0000	-
30. Wholesale and Retail Trade	6	-1.0000	-
31. Rail Transport	7A		-
32. Other Transport, Storage and Communication	7B	-1.0000	-
33. Finance, Insurance, and Real Estate	8	-1.0000	-
34. Commercial, Social and Personal Services	9	-1.0000	-

etar(j) : Demand elasticity of India's export of good j (unit : elasticity)

Table 7. Elasticity (Imports)

SN	SECTOR	ISIC Code	etam (j)	Source
1.	Paddy	1 A	-1.5800	Sinha , N . (1986)
2.	Wheat	1 B	-1.5800	Sinha , N . (1986)
3.	Other Cereals	1 C	-2.2831	Pohit (1995)
4.	Rest of Agriculture	1 D	-3.6050	Jayaraman , T . K . (1977)
5.	Food, Beverage and Tobacco	310	-1.3824	IEG - DSE (1994)
6.	Textiles	321	-2.2200	Patra & Ranjan (1992)
7.	Clothing	322	-2.2200	Patra & Ranjan (1992)
8.	Leather Products	323	-2.1250	Jayaraman , T . K . (1977)
9.	Footwear	324	-2.1250	Jayaraman , T . K . (1977)
10.	Wood Products	331	-2.1250	Jayaraman , T . K . (1977)
11.	Furniture Fixtures	332	-2.1250	Jayaraman , T . K . (1977)
12.	Paper Products	341	-0.7300	Patra & Ranjan (1992)
13.	Printing and Publishing	342	-1.9290	Jayaraman , T . K . (1977)
14.	Fertilizer	35 A	-0.9280	Jayaraman , T . K . (1977)
15.	Other Chemicals	35 B	-1.1690	Pohit and Bhide (1994)
16.	Petroleum Products	35 C	-0.1100	IEG - DSE (1994)
17.	Rubber Products	355	-2.1250	Jayaraman , T . K . (1977)
18.	Non-metallic Mineral Products	36 A	-2.1250	Jayaraman , T . K . (1977)
19.	Glass Products	362	-2.1250	Jayaraman , T . K . (1977)
20.	Iron and Steel	371	-1.1450	Patra & Ranjan (1992)
21.	Non-ferrous Metal	372	-1.1690	Pohit and Bhide (1994)
22.	Metal Products	381	-1.1690	Pohit and Bhide (1994)
23.	Non-electrical Machinery	382	-1.6330	Pohit and Bhide (1994)
24.	Electrical Machinery	383	-1.2700	Patra & Ranjan (1992)
25.	Transport Equipment	384	-1.6330	Pohit and Bhide (1994)
26.	Miscellaneous Manufacturing	38 A	-1.9290	Jayaraman . T . K . (1977)
27.	Mining and Quarrying	2	-1.0300	Patra & Ranjan (1992)
28.	Electricity, Gas and Water	4	-1.0000	-
29.	Construction	5	-1.0000	-
30.	Wholesale and Retail Trade	6	-1.0000	-
31.	Rail Transport	7A		-
32.	Other Transport, Storage and Communication	7B	-1.0000	-
33.	Finance, Insurance, and Real Estate	8	-1.0000	-
34.	Commercial, Social and Personal Services	9	-1.0000	-

etam (j) : Demand elasticity of India's Import of good j (unit : elasticity)

Table 8. Substitution Parameter between Factors of Production

SN SECTOR	ISIC Code	sigmabar1(j)	sigma (j) michigan	sigma (j) ours	sigma2(j)/ sigma3(j)
1. Paddy	1A		1.1387	1.6924	0.7800
2. Wheat	1B		1.1387	0.8987	0.7800
3. Other Cereals	1C		1.1387	1.0573	0.7800
4. Rest of Agriculture	1D		1.1387	1.5587	0.7800
5. Food, Beverage and Tobacco	310	0.5800	1.1345	1.6822	
6. Textiles	321	0.7700	1.1478	2.6855	
7. Clothing	322	1.2000	5.0163	2.2898	
8. Leather Products	323	1.0800	1.6687	7.2646	
9. Footwear	324	0.5000	4.5308	1.4966	
10. Wood Products	331	0.6800	1.7423	3.2310	
11. Furniture Fixtures	332	1.1220	3.2665	8.0076	
12. Paper Products	341	1.0100	1.5875	1.2640	
13. Printing and Publishing	342	0.9800	3.0149	18.9434	
14. Fertilizer	35A	0.7300	2.6171	1.4478	
15. Other Chemicals	35B	0.7300	2.6171	1.5939	
16. Petroleum Products	35C	1.8500	2.0022	4.4746	
17. Rubber Products	355	1.1700	5.6926	2.4282	
18. Non-metallic Mineral Products	36A	1.0500	2.8079	1.6592	
19. Glass Products	362	0.9000	1.6477	1.5560	
20. Iron and Steel	371	0.6400	1.4637	0.2710	
21. Non-ferrous Metal	372	0.9500	1.4319	3.2408	
22. Metal Products	381	1.0200	3.6993	1.5670	
23. Non-electrical Machinery	382	0.9100	1.0225	5.6975	
24. Electrical Machinery	383	0.7500	2.3423	1.2409	
25. Transport Equipment	384	0.4900	3.6805	1.8532	
26. Miscellaneous Manufacturing	38A	0.7700	1.9225	1.7107	
27. Mining and Quarrying	2	1.5410	1.6195	3.4096	
28. Electricity, Gas and Water	4	2.2660	2.1450	4.6925	
29. Construction	5	1.1050	2.1450	8.0380	
30. Wholesale and Retail Trade	6	2.2660	2.1450	2.2097	
31. Rail Transport	7A	1.4570			
32. Other Transport, Storage and Communication	7B	1.4570	2.1450	2.6177	
33. Finance, Insurance, and Real Estate	8	1.6570	2.1450	1.3549	
34. Commercial, Social and Personal Services	9	1.0870	2.1450	14.2933	

sigmabar1(j) : Elasticity of substitution between capital and labor (unit : elasticity)
sigma(j) : Elasticity of substitution between different varieties of good j (unit : elasticity)
sigma 2(j)/sigma3(j) : Elasticity of substitution between factors of production (unit : elasticity)

Table 9. Share of Factors

SN SECTOR	ISIC Code	hF(j)	Fo	hF(j)*Fo
1. Paddy	1A	0.1696		44.9079
2. Wheat	1B	0.0944		25.0079
3. Other Cereals	1C	0.1511		40.0127
4. Rest of Agriculture	1D	0.5849		154.8715
5. Food, Beverage and Tobacco	310			
6. Textiles	321			
7. Clothing	322			
8. Leather Products	323			
9. Footwear	324			
10. Wood Products	331			
11. Furniture Fixtures	332			
12. Paper Products	341			
13. Printing and Publishing	342			
14. Fertilizer	35A			
15. Other Chemicals	35B			
16. Petroleum Products	35C			
17. Rubber Products	355			
18. Non-metallic Mineral Products	36A			
19. Glass Products	362			
20. Iron and Steel	371			
21. Non-ferrous Metal	372			
22. Metal Products	381			
23. Non-electrical Machinery	382			
24. Electrical Machinery	383			
25. Transport Equipment	384			
26. Miscellaneous Manufacturing	38A			
27. Mining and Quarrying	2			
28. Electricity, Gas and Water	4			
29. Construction	5			
30. Wholesale and Retail Trade	6			
31. Rail Transport	7A			
32. Other Transport, Storage and Communication	7B			
33. Finance, Insurance, and Real Estate	8			
34. Commercial, Social and Personal Services	9			
Total		1	265	264.8000

hF(j) : Fraction of land in India allocated to sector j (unit : decimal fraction)
Fo : Total land stock (unit : thousand hectares)
hF(j)*Fo : Land allocated to agricultural sector (unit: thousand hectares)

SN	SECTOR	ISIC Code	hL(j)	Lo	hL(j)*Lo
1.	Paddy	1A	0.1717		51
2.	Wheat	1B	0.1272		38
3.	Other Cereals	1C	0.1717		51
4.	Rest of Agriculture	1D	0.1654		49
5.	Food, Beverage and Tobacco	310	0.0253		7
6.	Textiles	321	0.0223		7
7.	Clothing	322	0.0016		0
8.	Leather Products	323	0.0008		0
9.	Footwear	324	0.0007		0
10.	Wood Products	331	0.0011		0
11.	Furniture Fixtures	332	0.0001		0
12.	Paper Products	341	0.0021		1
13.	Printing and Publishing	342	0.0022		1
14.	Fertilizer	35A	0.0015		0
15.	Other Chemicals	35B	0.0067		2
16.	Petroleum Products	35C	0.0009		0
17.	Rubber Products	355	0.0017		1
18.	Non-metallic Mineral Products	36A	0.0060		2
19.	Glass Products	362	0.0009		0
20.	Iron and Steel	371	0.0065		2
21.	Non-ferrous Metal	372	0.0027		1
22.	Metal Products	381	0.0035		1
23.	Non-electrical Machinery	382	0.0073		2
24.	Electrical Machinery	383	0.0057		2
25.	Transport Equipment	384	0.0093		3
26.	Miscellaneous Manufacturing	38A	0.0032		1
27.	Mining and Quarrying	2	0.0080		2
28.	Electricity, Gas and Water	4	0.0038		1
29.	Construction	5	0.0403		12
30.	Wholesale and Retail Trade	6	0.0747		22
31.	Rail Transport	7A	0.0061		2
32.	Other Transport, Storage and Communication	7B	0.0220		6
33.	Finance, Insurance, and Real Estate	8	0.0084		2
34.	Commercial, Social and Personal Services	9	0.0886		26
	Total		1	295	295

hL(j) : Fraction of labor employed in sector j (unit : decimal fraction)
Lo : Total labour force (unit : number in millions)
hL(j)* Lo : Labour force employed in sector j (unit: number in millions)

Table 10. Firms

SN	SECTOR	ISIC Code	n(j)
1.	Paddy	1A	
2.	Wheat	1B	
3.	Other Cereals	1C	
4.	Rest of Agriculture	1D	
5.	Food, Beverage and Tobacco	310	28430
6.	Textiles	321	12430
7.	Clothing	322	1544
8.	Leather Products	323	839
9.	Footwear	324	284
10.	Wood Products	331	3196
11.	Furniture Fixtures	332	325
12.	Paper Products	341	1967
13.	Printing and Publishing	342	3131
14.	Fertilizer	35A	556
15.	Other Chemicals	35B	5255
16.	Petroleum Products	35C	1
17.	Rubber Products	355	1908
18.	Non-metallic Mineral Products	36A	8412
19.	Glass Products	362	626
20.	Iron and Steel	371	1
21.	Non-ferrous Metal	372	2737
22.	Metal Products	381	6683
23.	Non-electrical Machinery	382	8079
24.	Electrical Machinery	383	4658
25.	Transport Equipment	384	4830
26.	Miscellaneous Manufacturing	38A	5165
27.	Mining and Quarrying	2	1
28.	Electricity, Gas and Water	4	1
29.	Construction	5	
30.	Wholesale and Retail Trade	6	
31.	Rail Transport	7A	
32.	Other Transport, Storage and Communication	7B	
33.	Finance, Insurance, and Real Estate	8	
34.	Commercial, Social and Personal Services	9	
	Total		101059

n (j) : Number of firms in sector j (unit : integer)

Table 11. Values

SN	SECTOR	ISIC Code	S(j)	demand_fm(j)	demand_dm(j)
1.	Paddy	1A	305273	252196	251189
2.	Wheat	1B	153795	116422	116617
3.	Other Cereals	1C	75998	68390	68606
4.	Rest of Agriculture	1D	1274741	698123	686004
5.	Food, Beverage and Tobacco	310	347930	278829	272976
6.	Textiles	321	519963	337232	317019
7.	Clothing	322	88864	79399	36851
8.	Leather Products	323	17917	10884	1100
9.	Footwear	324	18285	18248	13028
10.	Wood Products	331	24281	2481	2695
11.	Furniture Fixtures	332	3471	1724	1720
12.	Paper Products	341	49211	-5337	4184
13.	Printing and Publishing	342	36711	18269	19154
14.	Fertilizer	35A	62294	-9474	2790
15.	Other Chemicals	35B	253450	59811	87714
16.	Petroleum Products	35C	173382	42875	52895
17.	Rubber Products	355	45742	26233	20097
18.	Non-metallic Mineral Products	36A	58917	29368	470
19.	Glass Products	362	49087	31072	9307
20.	Iron and Steel	371	177158	-15657	12704
21.	Non-ferrous Metal	372	37334	-12615	538
22.	Metal Products	381	66688	10043	21716
23.	Non-electrical Machinery	382	135705	85703	163264
24.	Electrical Machinery	383	168684	101687	125121
25.	Transport Equipment	384	161818	95029	109220
26.	Miscellaneous Manufacturing	38A	120160	66218	74900
27.	Mining and Quarrying	2	130772	-82069	8041
28.	Electricity, Gas and Water	4	215171	30170	30103
29.	Construction	5	561964	460356	456026
30.	Wholesale and Retail Trade	6	614688	320832	274179
31.	Rail Transport	7A	100802	50412	50412
32.	Other Transport, Storage and Communication	7B	365920	178047	184144
33.	Finance, Insurance, and Real Estate	8	405957	276723	273479
34.	Commercial, Social and Personal Services	9	761316	592462	586792

S (j) : Production of good j (unit : Rs. Million)
demand_fm(j) : Final demand for sector j (Unit : Rs. million)
demand_dm(j) : Domestic demand for sector j (Unit : Rs. million)

Table 12. Various Demands

SN SECTOR	ISIC Code	Di (j)	Di(j)/n(j)	Dm (j)	Dr (j)	E(j)
1. Paddy	1A	301437	0	2829	3836	304266
2. Wheat	1B	153776	0	214	19	153990
3. Other Cereals	1C	75979	0	235	19	76214
4. Rest of Agriculture	1D	1249623	0	12999	25118	1262622
5. Food, Beverage and Tobacco	310	337016	12	5061	10914	342077
6. Textiles	321	496194	40	3557	23770	499751
7. Clothing	322	45658	30	659	43206	46317
8. Leather Products	323	7896	9	237	10021	8132
9. Footwear	324	12988	46	77	5297	13065
10. Wood Products	331	24143	8	351	138	24494
11. Furniture Fixtures	332	3467	11	0	3	3467
12. Paper Products	341	49053	25	9678	158	58731
13. Printing and Publishing	342	36621	12	975	90	37596
14. Fertilizer	35A	62279	112	12279	15	74558
15. Other Chemicals	35B	237421	45	43932	16029	281353
16. Petroleum Products	35C	168079	168079	15323	5303	183402
17. Rubber Products	355	38977	20	629	6765	39606
18. Non-metallic Mineral Products	36A	29842	4	178	29076	30019
19. Glass Products	362	25788	41	1534	23298	27322
20. Iron and Steel	371	174900	174900	30619	2258	205519
21. Non-ferrous Metal	372	36428	13	14059	906	50487
22. Metal Products	381	65595	10	12766	1093	78360
23. Non-electrical Machinery	382	122672	15	90594	13033	213266
24. Electrical Machinery	383	158624	34	33494	10060	192118
25. Transport Equipment	384	154605	32	21404	7213	176009
26. Miscellaneous Manufacturing	38A	114823	22	14019	5338	128842
27. Mining and Quarrying	2	125784	125784	95098	4988	220882
28. Electricity, Gas and Water	4	215104	215104	0	67	215104
29. Construction	5	553515	0	4119	8449	557633
30. Wholesale and Retail Trade	6	558642	0	9393	56046	568035
31. Rail Transport	7A	100802	0	0	0	100802
32. Other Transport, Storage and Communication	7B	323305	0	48712	42615	372017
33. Finance, Insurance, and Real Estate	8	398914	0	3799	7042	402713
34. Commercial, Social and Personal Services	9	755439	0	207	5877	755646

Di(j) : Demand of jth good produced by a representative industry in India by India (unit : Rs. mlllions).
Di(j)/n(j) : Demand of jth good produced by a representative firm in India by India (unit : Rs. mlllions per firm).
Dm(j) : Imported demand of good j produced by ROW (unit : Rs. millions)
Dr(j) : Demand of j th good produced by a representative firm/industry in India by ROW (unit : Rs. Millions).
E (j) : Aggregate expenditure on good j (unit : Rs. millions)

Table 13. Taxes

SN SECTOR	ISIC Code	t(j) 1989-90	t(j) 1990-91	t(j) average	tx(j)	nt (j)
1. Paddy	1A	0.0000	0.0000	0.0000	0.0000	-0.0366
2. Wheat	1B	0.0000	0.0000	0.0000	0.0000	-0.0533
3. Other Cereals	1C	0.0365	0.0000	0.0182	0.0000	-0.0166
4. Rest of Agriculture	1D	0.2805	0.3504	0.3154	0.0053	-0.0146
5. Food, Beverage and Tobacco	310	0.3072	0.4735	0.3903	0.0183	0.0327
6. Textiles	321	0.5899	0.8105	0.7002	0.0000	0.0377
7. Clothing	322	0.1748	0.1125	0.1436	0.0000	0.0126
8. Leather Products	323	0.0394	0.6507	0.3450	0.0000	0.0269
9. Footwear	324	0.3753	0.3159	0.3456	0.0000	0.0437
10. Wood Products	331	0.2981	0.1625	0.2303	0.0000	0.0268
11. Furniture Fixtures	332	1.3650	1.1708	1.2679	0.0000	0.0219
12. Paper Products	341	0.1812	0.2080	0.1946	0.0000	0.0140
13. Printing and Publishing	342	0.2836	0.0607	0.1721	0.0000	0.0476
14. Fertilizer	35A	0.0064	0.0341	0.0203	0.0000	0.0092
15. Other Chemicals	35B	0.9233	0.9237	0.9235	0.0000	-0.0384
16. Petroleum Products	35C	0.1712	0.1802	0.1757	0.0000	0.2428
17. Rubber Products	355	0.9204	0.9000	0.9102	0.0000	0.0911
18. Non-metallic Mineral Products	36A	0.8982	0.8818	0.8900	0.0000	0.0441
19. Glass Products	362	0.5428	0.6154	0.5791	0.0000	0.0715
20. Iron and Steel	371	0.5037	0.6843	0.5940	0.0000	-0.0020
21. Non-ferrous Metal	372	1.1674	0.5591	0.8632	0.0000	-0.1619
22. Metal Products	381	0.5939	0.5940	0.5940	0.0000	0.0029
23. Non-electrical Machinery	382	0.5220	0.5858	0.5539	0.0000	-0.2299
24. Electrical Machinery	383	0.7871	0.8887	0.8379	0.0000	-0.0278
25. Transport Equipment	384	0.3236	0.2796	0.3016	0.0000	0.0573
26. Miscellaneous Manufacturing	38A	0.1114	0.1149	0.1132	0.0000	0.1120
27. Mining and Quarrying	2	0.4191	0.3959	0.4075	0.0200	-0.2163
28. Electricity, Gas and Water	4	0.0000	0.0000	0.0000	0.0000	0.0271
29. Construction	5	0.0000	0.0000	0.0000	0.0000	0.0644
30. Wholesale and Retail Trade	6	0.0000	0.0000	0.0000	0.0000	0.0054
31. Rail Transport	7A					0.0325
32. Other Transport, Storage and Communication	7B	0.0000	0.0000	0.0000	0.0000	0.0705
33. Finance, Insurance, and Real Estate	8	0.0000	0.0000	0.0000	0.0000	0.0020
34. Commercial, Social and Personal Services	9	0.0000	0.0000	0.0000	0.0000	0.0177

nt(j) : Net production tax in sector j (unit : decimal fraction)
tx(j) : Export tax imposed by India on its export of good j (unit : decimal fraction)
t(j) : Tariff imposed by India on imports of good j (unit : decimal fraction)

Table 14. Quotas

SN SECTOR	ISIC Code	thetaMQ(j)	thetaXQ(j)
1. Paddy	1A	0.8000	0.8000
2. Wheat	1B	0.8000	0.8000
3. Other Cereals	1C	0.8000	0.8000
4. Rest of Agriculture	1D	0.5000	0.6000
5. Food, Beverage and Tobacco	310	0.8000	0.2000
6. Textiles	321	0.5000	0.5000
7. Clothing	322	0.5000	0.5000
8. Leather Products	323	0.8000	0.5000
9. Footwear	324	0.8000	0.5000
10. Wood Products	331	0.5000	0.5000
11. Furniture Fixtures	332	0.5000	0.3000
12. Paper Products	341	0.7500	0.3000
13. Printing and Publishing	342	0.8000	0.3000
14. Fertilizer	35A	0.8000	0.8000
15. Other Chemicals	35B	0.2500	0.3000
16. Petroleum Products	35C	0.2500	0.8000
17. Rubber Products	355	0.2500	0.2000
18. Non-metallic Mineral Products	36A	0.2500	0.5000
19. Glass Products	362	0.2500	0.2000
20. Iron and Steel	371	0.2500	0.6000
21. Non-ferrous Metal	372	0.2500	0.5000
22. Metal Products	381	0.2500	0.2000
23. Non-electrical Machinery	382	0.5000	0.2000
24. Electrical Machinery	383	0.5000	0.2000
25. Transport Equipment	384	0.7500	0.2000
26. Miscellaneous Manufacturing	38A	0.8000	0.2000
27. Mining and Quarrying	2	0.8000	0.8000
28. Electricity, Gas and Water	4	0.8000	0.8000
29. Construction	5	0.8000	0.5000
30. Wholesale and Retail Trade	6	0.8000	0.8000
31. Rail Transport	7A		
32. Other Transport, Storage and Communication	7B	0.8000	0.8000
33. Finance, Insurance, and Real Estate	8	0.8000	0.8000
34. Commercial, Social and Personal Services	9	0.8000	0.8000

thetaMQ(j): Fractions of imp. of goods j by India that are subjected to QR (unit : decimal fraction).
thetaXQ(j): Fractions of exp. of goods j by India subjected to QR (unit: decimal fraction)

Table 15. Demand Share Parameters

SN SECTOR	ISIC Code	thetaI(j)	thetaM(j)	Total
1. Paddy	1A	0.9907	0.0093	1.0000
2. Wheat	1B	0.9986	0.0014	1.0000
3. Other Cereals	1C	0.9969	0.0031	1.0000
4. Rest of Agriculture	1D	0.9897	0.0103	1.0000
5. Food, Beverage and Tobacco	310	0.9852	0.0148	1.0000
6. Textiles	321	0.9929	0.0071	1.0000
7. Clothing	322	0.9858	0.0142	1.0000
8. Leather Products	323	0.9709	0.0291	1.0000
9. Footwear	324	0.9941	0.0059	1.0000
10. Wood Products	331	0.9857	0.0143	1.0000
11. Furniture Fixtures	332	1.0000	0.0000	1.0000
12. Paper Products	341	0.8352	0.1648	1.0000
13. Printing and Publishing	342	0.9741	0.0259	1.0000
14. Fertilizer	35A	0.8353	0.1647	1.0000
15. Other Chemicals	35B	0.8439	0.1561	1.0000
16. Petroleum Products	35C	0.9165	0.0835	1.0000
17. Rubber Products	355	0.9841	0.0159	1.0000
18. Non-metallic Mineral Products	36A	0.9941	0.0059	1.0000
19. Glass Products	362	0.9438	0.0562	1.0000
20. Iron and Steel	371	0.8510	0.1490	1.0000
21. Non-ferrous Metal	372	0.7215	0.2785	1.0000
22. Metal Products	381	0.8371	0.1629	1.0000
23. Non-electrical Machinery	382	0.5752	0.4248	1.0000
24. Electrical Machinery	383	0.8257	0.1743	1.0000
25. Transport Equipment	384	0.8784	0.1216	1.0000
26. Miscellaneous Manufacturing	38A	0.8912	0.1088	1.0000
27. Mining and Quarrying	2	0.5695	0.4305	1.0000
28. Electricity, Gas and Water	4	1.0000	0.0000	1.0000
29. Construction	5	0.9926	0.0074	1.0000
30. Wholesale and Retail Trade	6	0.9835	0.0165	1.0000
31. Rail Transport	7A	1.0000	0.0000	1.0000
32. Other Transport, Storage and Communication	7B	0.8691	0.1309	1.0000
33. Finance, Insurance, and Real Estate	8	0.9906	0.0094	1.0000
34. Commercial, Social and Personal Services	9	0.9997	0.0003	1.0000

thetaI(j): Fraction of expenditure in India on home good j (unit : decimal fraction)
thetaM(j): Fraction of expenditure in India on imported good j (unit: decimal fraction)

Table 16. Input - Output Coefficients

SN SECTOR	ISIC Code	1	2	3	4	5	6	7	8	9
1. Paddy	1A	0.1110	0.0003	0.0000	0.0053	0.0042	0.0000	0.0007	0.0000	0.0000
2. Wheat	1B	0.0004	0.1297	0.0000	0.0062	0.0106	0.0001	0.0000	0.0000	0.0000
3. Other Cereals	1C	0.0001	0.0001	0.0133	0.0045	0.0024	0.0000	0.0000	0.0000	0.0000
4. Rest of Agriculture	1D	0.0786	0.0606	0.1243	0.1896	0.3879	0.1346	0.0000	0.2683	0.0235
5. Food, Beverage and Tobacco	310	0.0002	0.0001	0.0000	0.0095	0.1220	0.0010	0.0000	0.0106	0.0000
6. Textiles	321	0.0014	0.0007	0.0000	0.0032	0.0109	0.2466	0.1998	0.0137	0.0404
7. Clothing	322	0.0000	0.0000	0.0000	0.0000	0.0000	0.0001	0.0367	0.0000	0.0000
8. Leather Products	323	0.0000	0.0000	0.0000	0.0000	0.0000	0.0001	0.0000	0.1366	0.2144
9. Footwear	324	0.0000	0.0000	0.0000	0.0000	0.0000	0.0000	0.0000	0.0000	0.0009
10. Wood Products	331	0.0000	0.0000	0.0000	0.0000	0.0014	0.0022	0.0003	0.0034	0.0014
11. Furniture Fixtures	332	0.0000	0.0000	0.0000	0.0000	0.0000	0.0000	0.0000	0.0000	0.0006
12. Paper Products	341	0.0001	0.0001	0.0000	0.0001	0.0076	0.0058	0.0040	0.0020	0.0117
13. Printing and Publishing	342	0.0000	0.0000	0.0000	0.0001	0.0000	0.0002	0.0000	0.0000	0.0000
14. Fertilizer	35A	0.0547	0.0681	0.0357	0.0268	0.0001	0.0000	0.0000	0.0000	0.0000
15. Other Chemicals	35B	0.0038	0.0023	0.0004	0.0069	0.0160	0.0488	0.0008	0.0647	0.0206
16. Petroleum Products	35C	0.0140	0.0143	0.0131	0.0077	0.0104	0.0125	0.0042	0.0055	0.0035
17. Rubber Products	355	0.0000	0.0000	0.0000	0.0001	0.0000	0.0001	0.0003	0.0012	0.1027
18. Non-metallic Mineral Products	36A	0.0000	0.0000	0.0000	0.0000	0.0000	0.0000	0.0000	0.0000	0.0000
19. Glass Products	362	0.0000	0.0000	0.0000	0.0000	0.0023	0.0000	0.0000	0.0016	0.0000
20. Iron and Steel	371	0.0000	0.0000	0.0000	0.0000	0.0007	0.0008	0.0000	0.0006	0.0001
21. Non-ferrous Metal	372	0.0000	0.0000	0.0000	0.0000	0.0004	0.0014	0.0000	0.0009	0.0000
22. Metal Products	381	0.0005	0.0003	0.0000	0.0005	0.0162	0.0052	0.0090	0.0059	0.0074
23. Non-electrical Machinery	382	0.0055	0.0069	0.0084	0.0030	0.0032	0.0046	0.0041	0.0018	0.0020
24. Electrical Machinery	383	0.0000	0.0000	0.0000	0.0000	0.0000	0.0000	0.0000	0.0001	0.0000
25. Transport Equipment	384	0.0008	0.0012	0.0026	0.0013	0.0000	0.0000	0.0000	0.0001	0.0000
26. Miscellaneous Manufacturing	38A	0.0001	0.0001	0.0000	0.0003	0.0044	0.0023	0.0227	0.0024	0.0077
27. Mining and Quarrying	2	0.0005	0.0019	0.0000	0.0002	0.0078	0.0065	0.0040	0.0016	0.0022
28. Electricity, Gas and Water	4	0.0085	0.0333	0.0030	0.0042	0.0105	0.0516	0.0182	0.0094	0.0086
29. Construction	5	0.0255	0.0256	0.0410	0.0151	0.0060	0.0028	0.0075	0.0060	0.0047
30. Wholesale and Retail Trade	6	0.0230	0.0228	0.0102	0.0313	0.0823	0.0680	0.0407	0.0966	0.1156
31. Rail Transport	7A	0.0050	0.0071	0.0027	0.0028	0.0038	0.0028	0.0015	0.0019	0.0012
32. Other Transport, Storage and Communication	7B	0.0091	0.0093	0.0052	0.0092	0.0255	0.0323	0.0000	0.0588	0.0000
33. Finance, Insurance, and Real Estate	8	0.0076	0.0063	0.0087	0.0061	0.0178	0.0214	0.0000	0.0724	0.0000
34. Commercial, Social and Personal Services	9	0.0030	0.0017	0.0000	0.0023	0.0318	0.0531	0.0000	0.0637	0.0000

SN SECTOR	ISIC Code	10	11	12	13	14	15	16	17	18
1. Paddy	1A	0.0000	0.0000	0.0000	0.0000	0.0001	0.0087	0.0000	0.0000	0.0009
2. Wheat	1B	0.0000	0.0000	0.0001	0.0000	0.0000	0.0003	0.0000	0.0000	0.0003
3. Other Cereals	1C	0.0000	0.0000	0.0000	0.0000	0.0000	0.0000	0.0000	0.0000	0.0000
4. Rest of Agriculture	1D	0.5754	0.1148	0.0437	0.0002	0.0005	0.0259	0.0005	0.0929	0.0096
5. Food, Beverage and Tobacco	310	0.0001	0.0000	0.0027	0.0000	0.0003	0.0196	0.0001	0.0001	0.0004
6. Textiles	321	0.0011	0.0166	0.0118	0.0079	0.0310	0.0157	0.0009	0.0544	0.0417
7. Clothing	322	0.0000	0.0000	0.0022	0.0000	0.0000	0.0000	0.0000	0.0000	0.0000
8. Leather Products	323	0.0002	0.0005	0.0000	0.0003	0.0000	0.0000	0.0000	0.0037	0.0000
9. Footwear	324	0.0000	0.0000	0.0000	0.0000	0.0000	0.0000	0.0000	0.0000	0.0000
10. Wood Products	331	0.0112	0.1448	0.0006	0.0006	0.0002	0.0024	0.0002	0.0006	0.0003
11. Furniture Fixtures	332	0.0001	0.0867	0.0000	0.0000	0.0000	0.0000	0.0000	0.0000	0.0000
12. Paper Products	341	0.0002	0.0057	0.2814	0.4253	0.0014	0.0288	0.0010	0.0043	0.0011
13. Printing and Publishing	342	0.0001	0.0000	0.0028	0.0064	0.0000	0.0001	0.0000	0.0000	0.0000
14. Fertilizer	35A	0.0000	0.0000	0.0000	0.0000	0.1072	0.0004	0.0000	0.0000	0.0000
15. Other Chemicals	35B	0.0044	0.0068	0.0474	0.0280	0.1312	0.2207	0.0191	0.1487	0.0044
16. Petroleum Products	35C	0.0030	0.0023	0.0151	0.0044	0.1339	0.0324	0.0964	0.0109	0.0420
17. Rubber Products	355	0.0002	0.0012	0.0000	0.0005	0.0000	0.0004	0.0000	0.1066	0.0009
18. Non-metallic Mineral Products	36A	0.0000	0.0000	0.0000	0.0003	0.0000	0.0001	0.0000	0.0000	0.0066
19. Glass Products	362	0.0003	0.0000	0.0000	0.0009	0.0002	0.0047	0.0000	0.0015	0.0046
20. Iron and Steel	371	0.0016	0.0053	0.0010	0.0022	0.0001	0.0010	0.0000	0.0051	0.0120
21. Non-ferrous Metal	372	0.0004	0.0020	0.0279	0.0000	0.0005	0.0098	0.0000	0.0016	0.0088
22. Metal Products	381	0.0025	0.0131	0.0115	0.0092	0.0076	0.0293	0.0094	0.0161	0.0124
23. Non-electrical Machinery	382	0.0022	0.0000	0.0040	0.0069	0.0035	0.0032	0.0003	0.0015	0.0058
24. Electrical Machinery	383	0.0001	0.0000	0.0001	0.0000	0.0000	0.0000	0.0000	0.0001	0.0000
25. Transport Equipment	384	0.0003	0.0000	0.0001	0.0000	0.0000	0.0000	0.0000	0.0015	0.0000
26. Miscellaneous Manufacturing	38A	0.0016	0.0229	0.0026	0.0101	0.0059	0.0098	0.0016	0.0034	0.0022
27. Mining and Quarrying	2	0.0014	0.0018	0.0482	0.0007	0.1008	0.0528	0.4767	0.0064	0.2099
28. Electricity, Gas and Water	4	0.0036	0.0056	0.0571	0.0207	0.0890	0.0392	0.0054	0.0097	0.0525
29. Construction	5	0.0047	0.0004	0.0037	0.0026	0.0042	0.0040	0.0016	0.0060	0.0089
30. Wholesale and Retail Trade	6	0.0748	0.0441	0.0490	0.0431	0.0837	0.0689	0.0443	0.0906	0.0828
31. Rail Transport	7A	0.0047	0.0020	0.0130	0.0028	0.0176	0.0137	0.0041	0.0019	0.0309
32. Other Transport, Storage and Communication	7B	0.0265	0.0294	0.0371	0.0000	0.0245	0.0289	0.0094	0.0234	0.0455
33. Finance, Insurance, and Real Estate	8	0.0011	0.0016	0.0707	0.0000	0.0425	0.0269	0.0202	0.0231	0.0279
34. Commercial, Social and Personal Services	9	0.0124	0.0949	0.0517	0.0000	0.0209	0.0314	0.0022	0.0199	0.0792

(continued)

Table 16. *(Continued)*

SN SECTOR	ISIC Code	19	20	21	22	23	24	25	26	27
1. Paddy	1A	0.0000	0.0000	0.0000	0.0000	0.0000	0.0000	0.0000	0.0001	0.0000
2. Wheat	1B	0.0000	0.0000	0.0000	0.0000	0.0000	0.0000	0.0000	0.0000	0.0000
3. Other Cereals	1C	0.0000	0.0000	0.0000	0.0000	0.0000	0.0000	0.0000	0.0000	0.0000
4. Rest of Agriculture	1D	0.0033	0.0015	0.0008	0.0007	0.0036	0.0003	0.0021	0.0049	0.0000
5. Food, Beverage and Tobacco	310	0.0000	0.0000	0.0000	0.0000	0.0000	0.0000	0.0001	0.0003	0.0000
6. Textiles	321	0.0037	0.0009	0.0010	0.0021	0.0010	0.0009	0.0011	0.0061	0.0001
7. Clothing	322	0.0000	0.0000	0.0000	0.0000	0.0000	0.0000	0.0000	0.0002	0.0000
8. Leather Products	323	0.0000	0.0000	0.0000	0.0000	0.0001	0.0000	0.0002	0.0005	0.0000
9. Footwear	324	0.0000	0.0000	0.0000	0.0000	0.0000	0.0000	0.0000	0.0000	0.0000
10. Wood Products	331	0.0029	0.0002	0.0005	0.0018	0.0019	0.0027	0.0008	0.0028	0.0008
11. Furniture Fixtures	332	0.0000	0.0000	0.0000	0.0000	0.0000	0.0000	0.0000	0.0004	0.0000
12. Paper Products	341	0.0092	0.0003	0.0005	0.0055	0.0019	0.0077	0.0043	0.0076	0.0040
13. Printing and Publishing	342	0.0000	0.0000	0.0000	0.0000	0.0000	0.0000	0.0000	0.0011	0.0005
14. Fertilizer	35A	0.0000	0.0000	0.0000	0.0000	0.0000	0.0000	0.0000	0.0002	0.0000
15. Other Chemicals	35B	0.0322	0.0372	0.0279	0.0121	0.0104	0.0187	0.0114	0.0429	0.0181
16. Petroleum Products	35C	0.0587	0.0222	0.0539	0.0138	0.0082	0.0068	0.0158	0.0074	0.0268
17. Rubber Products	355	0.0000	0.0001	0.0001	0.0004	0.0057	0.0014	0.0245	0.0030	0.0002
18. Non-metallic Mineral Products	36A	0.0444	0.0010	0.0000	0.0000	0.0001	0.0000	0.0000	0.0000	0.0016
19. Glass Products	362	0.0561	0.0015	0.0003	0.0000	0.0001	0.0021	0.0014	0.0058	0.0024
20. Iron and Steel	371	0.0247	0.2175	0.0391	0.2729	0.1793	0.0632	0.1176	0.0420	0.0000
21. Non-ferrous Metal	372	0.0000	0.0366	0.1706	0.0000	0.0274	0.0810	0.0219	0.0755	0.0000
22. Metal Products	381	0.0138	0.0800	0.0205	0.0049	0.0254	0.0135	0.0227	0.0097	0.0066
23. Non-electrical Machinery	382	0.0030	0.0037	0.0014	0.0058	0.1387	0.0030	0.0125	0.0043	0.0611
24. Electrical Machinery	383	0.0009	0.0010	0.0061	0.0005	0.0205	0.1587	0.0148	0.0211	0.0000
25. Transport Equipment	384	0.0000	0.0008	0.0002	0.0000	0.0052	0.0011	0.1386	0.0191	0.0046
26. Miscellaneous Manufacturing	38A	0.0049	0.0010	0.0019	0.0006	0.0106	0.0257	0.0087	0.0975	0.0105
27. Mining and Quarrying	2	0.0928	0.0611	0.1338	0.0151	0.0016	0.0006	0.0036	0.0051	0.0091
28. Electricity, Gas and Water	4	0.0224	0.0446	0.1237	0.0352	0.0154	0.0104	0.0174	0.0165	0.0573
29. Construction	5	0.0085	0.0103	0.0052	0.0069	0.0068	0.0047	0.0163	0.0034	0.0178
30. Wholesale and Retail Trade	6	0.0661	0.0573	0.0461	0.0422	0.0386	0.0320	0.0322	0.0310	0.0146
31. Rail Transport	7A	0.0221	0.0223	0.0089	0.0144	0.0074	0.0036	0.0055	0.0036	0.0158
32. Other Transport, Storage and Communication	7B	0.0000	0.0193	0.0219	0.0000	0.0185	0.0141	0.0122	0.0334	0.0080
33. Finance, Insurance, and Real Estate	8	0.0000	0.0196	0.0403	0.0000	0.0234	0.0210	0.0188	0.0147	0.0155
34. Commercial, Social and Personal Services	9	0.0000	0.0238	0.0223	0.0000	0.0756	0.0323	0.0376	0.0754	0.0342

SN SECTOR	ISIC Code	28	29	30	31	32	33	34
1. Paddy	1A	0.0000	0.0000	0.0001	0.0000	0.0002	0.0000	0.0111
2. Wheat	1B	0.0000	0.0000	0.0000	0.0000	0.0003	0.0000	0.0071
3. Other Cereals	1C	0.0000	0.0000	0.0000	0.0000	0.0001	0.0000	0.0000
4. Rest of Agriculture	1D	0.0014	0.0324	0.0016	0.0001	0.0020	0.0000	0.0416
5. Food, Beverage and Tobacco	310	0.0000	0.0000	0.0004	0.0000	0.0018	0.0000	0.0100
6. Textiles	321	0.0000	0.0020	0.0028	0.0007	0.0010	0.0000	0.0137
7. Clothing	322	0.0004	0.0001	0.0000	0.0001	0.0002	0.0000	0.0076
8. Leather Products	323	0.0000	0.0000	0.0001	0.0000	0.0000	0.0000	0.0003
9. Footwear	324	0.0000	0.0000	0.0000	0.0000	0.0001	0.0000	0.0000
10. Wood Products	331	0.0012	0.0272	0.0021	0.0004	0.0000	0.0000	0.0000
11. Furniture Fixtures	332	0.0000	0.0000	0.0000	0.0001	0.0000	0.0000	0.0017
12. Paper Products	341	0.[illegible]009	0.0005	0.0034	0.0018	0.0021	0.0007	0.0031
13. Printing and Publishing	342	0.[illegible]005	0.0011	0.0025	0.0006	0.0044	0.0011	0.0174
14. Fertilizer	35A	0.[illegible]000	0.0009	0.0001	0.0000	0.0000	0.0000	0.0004
15. Other Chemicals	35B	0.[illegible]015	0.0347	0.0010	0.0001	0.0005	0.0000	0.0371
16. Petroleum Products	35C	0.[illegible]164	0.0010	0.0009	0.0444	0.0999	0.0004	0.0008
17. Rubber Products	355	0.[illegible]001	0.0004	0.0002	0.0000	0.0179	0.0001	0.0000
18. Non-metallic Mineral Products	36A	0.[illegible]000	0.0471	0.0001	0.0000	0.0000	0.0000	0.0000
19. Glass Products	362	0.[illegible]011	0.0179	0.0000	0.0019	0.0001	0.0000	0.0006
20. Iron and Steel	371	0.[illegible]035	0.1185	0.0018	0.0098	0.0071	0.0000	0.0003
21. Non-ferrous Metal	372	0.[illegible]002	0.0000	0.0005	0.0000	0.0000	0.0000	0.0018
22. Metal Products	381	0.[illegible]021	0.0005	0.0033	0.0206	0.0020	0.0000	0.0019
23. Non-electrical Machinery	382	0.[illegible]109	0.0015	0.0004	0.0021	0.0037	0.0008	0.0005
24. Electrical Machinery	383	0.[illegible]245	0.0356	0.0005	0.0175	0.0091	0.0002	0.0015
25. Transport Equipment	384	0.[illegible]003	0.0009	0.0006	0.1944	0.0440	0.0031	0.0002
26. Miscellaneous Manufacturing	38A	0.[illegible]117	0.0014	0.0027	0.0007	0.0045	0.0000	0.0225
27. Mining and Quarrying	2	0.[illegible]288	0.0534	0.0004	0.0195	0.0008	0.0000	0.0050
28. Electricity, Gas and Water	4	0.[illegible]479	0.0173	0.0085	0.0328	0.0123	0.0038	0.0076
29. Construction	5	0.[illegible]193	0.0001	0.0038	0.0782	0.0097	0.0682	0.0062
30. Wholesale and Retail Trade	6	0.[illegible]340	0.0776	0.0131	0.0137	0.0251	0.0014	0.0214
31. Rail Transport	7A	0.[illegible]320	0.0143	0.0030	0.0080	0.0066	0.0006	0.0018
32. Other Transport, Storage and Communication	7B	0.[illegible]140	0.0254	0.0854	0.0108	0.0639	0.0004	0.0229
33. Finance, Insurance, and Real Estate	8	0.[illegible]065	0.0114	0.0274	0.0319	0.0296	0.0014	0.0288
34. Commercial, Social and Personal Services	9	0.[illegible]050	0.0204	0.0438	0.0186	0.0241	0.0005	0.0208

iom (i,j) : Input-Output Coefficients (unit : decimal fraction)

Table 17. Cost Share Parameters

SN SECTOR	ISIC CODE	b0(j)	bt(j)
1. Paddy	1A	0.6831	-0.0366
2. Wheat	1B	0.6604	-0.0533
3. Other Cereals	1C	0.7480	-0.0166
4. Rest of Agriculture	1D	0.6754	-0.0118
5. Food, Beverage and Tobacco	310	0.1759	0.0378
6. Textiles	321	0.2536	0.0417
7. Clothing	322	0.6319	0.0135
8. Leather Products	323	0.1395	0.0307
9. Footwear	324	0.3858	0.0449
10. Wood Products	331	0.2313	0.0295
11. Furniture Fixtures	332	0.3754	0.0219
12. Paper Products	341	0.1690	0.0455
13. Printing and Publishing	342	0.3754	0.0514
14. Fertilizer	35A	0.1809	0.0124
15. Other Chemicals	35B	0.2276	0.0932
16. Petroleum Products	35C	0.0509	0.2555
17. Rubber Products	355	0.2648	0.1014
18. Non-metallic Mineral Products	36A	0.2623	0.0463
19. Glass Products	362	0.4438	0.0864
20. Iron and Steel	371	0.2540	0.0824
21. Non-ferrous Metal	372	0.1677	0.1053
22. Metal Products	381	0.4686	0.0963
23. Non-electrical Machinery	382	0.2985	0.0741
24. Electrical Machinery	383	0.3855	0.1089
25. Transport Equipment	384	0.3678	0.0901
26. Miscellaneous Manufacturing	38A	0.3416	0.1228
27. Mining and Quarrying	2	0.6625	0.0279
28. Electricity, Gas and Water	4	0.4086	0.0271
29. Construction	5	0.3918	0.0644
30. Wholesale and Retail Trade	6	0.7840	0.0054
31. Rail Transport	7A	0.4587	0.0325
32. Other Transport, Storage and Communication	7B	0.5566	0.0705
33. Finance, Insurance, and Real Estate	8	0.9152	0.0020
34. Commercial, Social and Personal Services	9	0.6863	0.0177

b0(j) : Primary input share of total cost in industry j in India (unit: decimal fraction)
bt(j) : Other tax net of subsidies share of total cost in industry j in India (unit: decimal fraction)

Table 18. Demand Shares

SN SECTOR	ISIC Code	v0(j)
1. Paddy	1A	0.8256
2. Wheat	1B	0.7573
3. Other Cereals	1C	0.9002
4. Rest of Agriculture	1D	0.5433
5. Food, Beverage and Tobacco	310	0.7980
6. Textiles	321	0.6344
7. Clothing	322	0.7957
8. Leather Products	323	0.1353
9. Footwear	324	0.9972
10. Wood Products	331	0.1100
11. Furniture Fixtures	332	0.4967
12. Paper Products	341	0.0712
13. Printing and Publishing	342	0.5095
14. Fertilizer	35A	0.0374
15. Other Chemicals	35B	0.3118
16. Petroleum Products	35C	0.2884
17. Rubber Products	355	0.5074
18. Non-metallic Mineral Products	36A	0.0157
19. Glass Products	362	0.3407
20. Iron and Steel	371	0.0618
21. Non-ferrous Metal	372	0.0107
22. Metal Products	381	0.2771
23. Non-electrical Machinery	382	0.7655
24. Electrical Machinery	383	0.6513
25. Transport Equipment	384	0.6205
26. Miscellaneous Manufacturing	38A	0.5813
27. Mining and Quarrying	2	0.0364
28. Electricity, Gas and Water	4	0.1399
29. Construction	5	0.8177
30. Wholesale and Retail Trade	6	0.4827
31. Rail Transport	7A	0.4583
32. Other Transport, Storage and Communication	7B	0.4950
33. Finance, Insurance, and Real Estate	8	0.6791
34. Commercial, Social and Personal Services	9	0.7765

v0(j) : Final demand share of total purchases of good j in India (unit : decimal fraction)

Table 19. Cost Shares

SN SECTOR	ISIC Code	1	2	3	4	5	6	7	8	9
1. Paddy	1A	0.1114	0.0001	0.0000	0.0222	0.0048	0.0001	0.0002	0.0000	0.0000
2. Wheat	1B	0.0008	0.1295	0.0000	0.0515	0.0239	0.0002	0.0000	0.0000	0.0000
3. Other Cereals	1C	0.0003	0.0002	0.0133	0.0745	0.0111	0.0000	0.0000	0.0000	0.0000
4. Rest of Agriculture	1D	0.0190	0.0074	0.0075	0.1915	0.1069	0.0554	0.0000	0.0038	0.0003
5. Food, Beverage and Tobacco	310	0.0002	0.0000	0.0000	0.0354	0.1241	0.0015	0.0000	0.0006	0.0000
6. Textiles	321	0.0009	0.0002	0.0000	0.0081	0.0076	0.2566	0.0355	0.0005	0.0015
7. Clothing	322	0.0000	0.0000	0.0000	0.0008	0.0000	0.0012	0.0705	0.0000	0.0000
8. Leather Products	323	0.0000	0.0000	0.0000	0.0000	0.0001	0.0094	0.0003	0.3010	0.4820
9. Footwear	324	0.0000	0.0000	0.0000	0.0000	0.0000	0.0000	0.0000	0.0000	0.0013
10. Wood Products	331	0.0001	0.0000	0.0000	0.0005	0.0201	0.0462	0.0009	0.0025	0.0010
11. Furniture Fixtures	332	0.0000	0.0000	0.0000	0.0031	0.0000	0.0001	0.0000	0.0000	0.0030
12. Paper Products	341	0.0004	0.0002	0.0000	0.0029	0.0448	0.0513	0.0061	0.0006	0.0036
13. Printing and Publishing	342	0.0003	0.0002	0.0000	0.0018	0.0001	0.0034	0.0000	0.0000	0.0000
14. Fertilizer	35A	0.2239	0.1405	0.0364	0.4580	0.0006	0.0000	0.0000	0.0000	0.0000
15. Other Chemicals	35B	0.0041	0.0013	0.0001	0.0312	0.0198	0.0902	0.0003	0.0041	0.0013
16. Petroleum Products	35C	0.0233	0.0120	0.0054	0.0534	0.0197	0.0353	0.0020	0.0005	0.0004
17. Rubber Products	355	0.0001	0.0001	0.0000	0.0029	0.0000	0.0012	0.0006	0.0005	0.0474
18. Non-metallic Mineral Products	36A	0.0000	0.0000	0.0000	0.0000	0.0000	0.0000	0.0000	0.0000	0.0000
19. Glass Products	362	0.0000	0.0000	0.0000	0.0001	0.0292	0.0002	0.0000	0.0011	0.0000
20. Iron and Steel	371	0.0000	0.0000	0.0000	0.0001	0.0012	0.0019	0.0000	0.0000	0.0000
21. Non-ferrous Metal	372	0.0000	0.0000	0.0000	0.0001	0.0029	0.0145	0.0000	0.0003	0.0000
22. Metal Products	381	0.0019	0.0005	0.0000	0.0086	0.0721	0.0347	0.0102	0.0013	0.0017
23. Non-electrical Machinery	382	0.0078	0.0050	0.0030	0.0182	0.0052	0.0112	0.0017	0.0002	0.0002
24. Electrical Machinery	383	0.0000	0.0000	0.0000	0.0003	0.0000	0.0000	0.0000	0.0000	0.0000
25. Transport Equipment	384	0.0014	0.0010	0.0011	0.0094	0.0000	0.0000	0.0000	0.0000	0.0000
26. Miscellaneous Manufacturing	38A	0.0002	0.0001	0.0000	0.0025	0.0118	0.0093	0.0157	0.0003	0.0011
27. Mining and Quarrying	2	0.0007	0.0014	0.0000	0.0014	0.0122	0.0152	0.0016	0.0001	0.0002
28. Electricity, Gas and Water	4	0.0121	0.0238	0.0011	0.0249	0.0170	0.1247	0.0075	0.0008	0.0007
29. Construction	5	0.0140	0.0071	0.0056	0.0346	0.0038	0.0026	0.0012	0.0002	0.0002
30. Wholesale and Retail Trade	6	0.0123	0.0062	0.0014	0.0702	0.0504	0.0623	0.0064	0.0030	0.0037
31. Rail Transport	7A	0.0153	0.0109	0.0021	0.0358	0.0132	0.0144	0.0013	0.0003	0.0002
32. Other Transport, Storage and Communication	7B	0.0075	0.0039	0.0011	0.0315	0.0238	0.0451	0.0000	0.0028	0.0000
33. Finance, Insurance, and Real Estate	8	0.0058	0.0024	0.0016	0.0192	0.0154	0.0276	0.0000	0.0032	0.0000
34. Commercial, Social and Personal Services	9	0.0012	0.0003	0.0000	0.0039	0.0146	0.0365	0.0000	0.0015	0.0000

vd(i,j) : Intermediate demand for good i by industry j's share of total purchases of good i in India (unit : decimal fraction)

SN SECTOR	ISIC Code	10	11	12	13	14	15	16	17	18
1. Paddy	1A	0.0000	0.0000	0.0000	0.0000	0.0000	0.0072	0.0000	0.0000	0.0002
2. Wheat	1B	0.0000	0.0000	0.0000	0.0000	0.0000	0.0005	0.0000	0.0000	0.0001
3. Other Cereals	1C	0.0000	0.0000	0.0000	0.0000	0.0000	0.0002	0.0000	0.0000	0.0000
4. Rest of Agriculture	1D	0.0111	0.0003	0.0017	0.0000	0.0000	0.0052	0.0001	0.0034	0.0004
5. Food, Beverage and Tobacco	310	0.0000	0.0000	0.0004	0.0000	0.0001	0.0145	0.0000	0.0000	0.0001
6. Textiles	321	0.0001	0.0001	0.0012	0.0006	0.0039	0.0080	0.0003	0.0050	0.0049
7. Clothing	322	0.0000	0.0000	0.0023	0.0000	0.0000	0.0000	0.0000	0.0000	0.0000
8. Leather Products	323	0.0006	0.0002	0.0000	0.0013	0.0000	0.0003	0.0000	0.0206	0.0000
9. Footwear	324	0.0000	0.0000	0.0000	0.0000	0.0000	0.0000	0.0000	0.0000	0.0000
10. Wood Products	331	0.0111	0.0205	0.0013	0.0009	0.0004	0.0249	0.0016	0.0012	0.0006
11. Furniture Fixtures	332	0.0010	0.0868	0.0000	0.0000	0.0000	0.0000	0.0000	0.0000	0.0000
12. Paper Products	341	0.0001	0.0003	0.2358	0.2658	0.0015	0.1243	0.0030	0.0034	0.0011
13. Printing and Publishing	342	0.0000	0.0000	0.0036	0.0062	0.0000	0.0004	0.0000	0.0000	0.0000
14. Fertilizer	35A	0.0000	0.0000	0.0000	0.0000	0.0895	0.0013	0.0000	0.0000	0.0000
15. Other Chemicals	35B	0.0004	0.0001	0.0083	0.0037	0.0291	0.1989	0.0118	0.0242	0.0009
16. Petroleum Products	35C	0.0004	0.0000	0.0040	0.0009	0.0455	0.0447	0.0911	0.0027	0.0135
17. Rubber Products	355	0.0001	0.0001	0.0000	0.0005	0.0000	0.0025	0.0000	0.1231	0.0013
18. Non-metallic Mineral Products	36A	0.0000	0.0000	0.0000	0.0004	0.0000	0.0008	0.0000	0.0000	0.0130
19. Glass Products	362	0.0003	0.0000	0.0000	0.0013	0.0004	0.0437	0.0000	0.0026	0.0100
20. Iron and Steel	371	0.0002	0.0001	0.0002	0.0004	0.0000	0.0012	0.0000	0.0011	0.0034
21. Non-ferrous Metal	372	0.0002	0.0001	0.0272	0.0000	0.0006	0.0491	0.0001	0.0014	0.0103
22. Metal Products	381	0.0008	0.0006	0.0072	0.0043	0.0060	0.0948	0.0208	0.0094	0.0093
23. Non-electrical Machinery	382	0.0003	0.0000	0.0009	0.0012	0.0010	0.0038	0.0003	0.0003	0.0016
24. Electrical Machinery	383	0.0000	0.0000	0.0000	0.0000	0.0000	0.0000	0.0000	0.0000	0.0000
25. Transport Equipment	384	0.0000	0.0000	0.0000	0.0000	0.0000	0.0000	0.0000	0.0004	0.0000
26. Miscellaneous Manufacturing	38A	0.0003	0.0006	0.0010	0.0029	0.0029	0.0193	0.0021	0.0012	0.0010
27. Mining and Quarrying	2	0.0002	0.0000	0.0107	0.0001	0.0284	0.0606	0.3742	0.0013	0.0560
28. Electricity, Gas and Water	4	0.0010	0.0001	0.0131	0.0035	0.0258	0.0462	0.0043	0.0021	0.0144
29. Construction	5	0.0002	0.0000	0.0003	0.0002	0.0005	0.0018	0.0005	0.0005	0.0009
30. Wholesale and Retail Trade	6	0.0032	0.0003	0.0042	0.0028	0.0092	0.0307	0.0135	0.0073	0.0086
31. Rail Transport	7A	0.0011	0.0001	0.0063	0.0010	0.0109	0.0345	0.0070	0.0008	0.0181
32. Other Transport, Storage and Communication	7B	0.0017	0.0003	0.0049	0.0000	0.0041	0.0197	0.0044	0.0029	0.0072
33. Finance, Insurance, and Real Estate	8	0.0001	0.0000	0.0086	0.0000	0.0066	0.0169	0.0087	0.0026	0.0041
34. Commercial, Social and Personal Services	9	0.0004	0.0004	0.0034	0.0000	0.0017	0.0105	0.0005	0.0012	0.0062

(continued)

Table 19. *(Continued)*

SN SECTOR	ISIC Code	19	20	21	22	23	24	25	26	27
1. Paddy	1A	0.0000	0.0000	0.0000	0.0000	0.0000	0.0000	0.0000	0.0000	0.0000
2. Wheat	1B	0.0000	0.0000	0.0000	0.0000	0.0000	0.0000	0.0000	0.0000	0.0000
3. Other Cereals	1C	0.0000	0.0000	0.0000	0.0000	0.0000	0.0000	0.0000	0.0000	0.0000
4. Rest of Agriculture	1D	0.0001	0.0002	0.0000	0.0000	0.0004	0.0000	0.0003	0.0005	0.0000
5. Food, Beverage and Tobacco	310	0.0000	0.0000	0.0000	0.0000	0.0000	0.0000	0.0000	0.0001	0.0000
6. Textiles	321	0.0004	0.0003	0.0001	0.0003	0.0003	0.0003	0.0004	0.0015	0.0000
7. Clothing	322	0.0000	0.0000	0.0000	0.0000	0.0000	0.0000	0.0000	0.0004	0.0000
8. Leather Products	323	0.0000	0.0002	0.0001	0.0003	0.0012	0.0002	0.0040	0.0080	0.0000
9. Footwear	324	0.0000	0.0000	0.0000	0.0000	0.0000	0.0000	0.0000	0.0000	0.0000
10. Wood Products	331	0.0057	0.0015	0.0008	0.0048	0.0106	0.0186	0.0050	0.0138	0.0043
11. Furniture Fixtures	332	0.0002	0.0000	0.0000	0.0004	0.0002	0.0004	0.0000	0.0127	0.0006
12. Paper Products	341	0.0077	0.0008	0.0003	0.0063	0.0043	0.0222	0.0119	0.0156	0.0089
13. Printing and Publishing	342	0.0000	0.0000	0.0000	0.0000	0.0000	0.0000	0.0000	0.0034	0.0017
14. Fertilizer	35A	0.0000	0.0000	0.0000	0.0000	0.0000	0.0000	0.0000	0.0003	0.0000
15. Other Chemicals	35B	0.0056	0.0234	0.0037	0.0029	0.0050	0.0112	0.0066	0.0183	0.0084
16. Petroleum Products	35C	0.0157	0.0215	0.0110	0.0050	0.0060	0.0063	0.0140	0.0048	0.0191
17. Rubber Products	355	0.0000	0.0005	0.0001	0.0007	0.0197	0.0062	0.1001	0.0091	0.0005
18. Non-metallic Mineral Products	36A	0.0725	0.0060	0.0000	0.0000	0.0006	0.0001	0.0001	0.0000	0.0071
19. Glass Products	362	0.1008	0.0097	0.0004	0.0000	0.0007	0.0130	0.0081	0.0254	0.0114
20. Iron and Steel	371	0.0059	0.1875	0.0071	0.0885	0.1184	0.0518	0.0926	0.0246	0.0000
21. Non-ferrous Metal	372	0.0000	0.1283	0.1261	0.0000	0.0736	0.2707	0.0702	0.1796	0.0000
22. Metal Products	381	0.0087	0.1808	0.0097	0.0042	0.0441	0.0290	0.0469	0.0149	0.0110
23. Non-electrical Machinery	382	0.0007	0.0031	0.0002	0.0018	0.0882	0.0024	0.0095	0.0024	0.0374
24. Electrical Machinery	383	0.0002	0.0009	0.0012	0.0002	0.0145	0.1394	0.0125	0.0132	0.0000
25. Transport Equipment	384	0.0000	0.0008	0.0000	0.0000	0.0040	0.0010	0.1275	0.0131	0.0034
26. Miscellaneous Manufacturing	38A	0.0019	0.0013	0.0006	0.0003	0.0112	0.0336	0.0109	0.0910	0.0106
27. Mining and Quarrying	2	0.0206	0.0490	0.0226	0.0046	0.0010	0.0005	0.0026	0.0028	0.0054
28. Electricity, Gas and Water	4	0.0051	0.0367	0.0215	0.0109	0.0097	0.0081	0.0131	0.0092	0.0349
29. Construction	5	0.0007	0.0033	0.0004	0.0008	0.0017	0.0014	0.0047	0.0007	0.0042
30. Wholesale and Retail Trade	6	0.0057	0.0179	0.0030	0.0050	0.0092	0.0095	0.0092	0.0066	0.0034
31. Rail Transport	7A	0.0108	0.0393	0.0033	0.0095	0.0099	0.0060	0.0089	0.0043	0.0205
32. Other Transport, Storage and Communication	7B	0.0000	0.0092	0.0022	0.0000	0.0067	0.0064	0.0053	0.0108	0.0028
33. Finance, Insurance, and Real Estate	8	0.0000	0.0086	0.0037	0.0000	0.0079	0.0088	0.0075	0.0044	0.0050
34. Commercial, Social and Personal Services	9	0.0000	0.0056	0.0011	0.0000	0.0136	0.0072	0.0080	0.0120	0.0059

SN SECTOR	ISIC Code	28	29	30	31	32	33	34
1. Paddy	1A	0.0000	0.0000	0.0002	0.0000	0.0002	0.0000	0.0278
2. Wheat	1B	0.0000	0.0000	0.0001	0.0000	0.0007	0.0000	0.0352
3. Other Cereals	1C	0.0000	0.0000	0.0001	0.0000	0.0003	0.0000	0.0000
4. Rest of Agriculture	1D	0.0002	0.0144	0.0008	0.0000	0.0006	0.0000	0.0251
5. Food, Beverage and Tobacco	310	0.0000	0.0000	0.0007	0.0000	0.0019	0.0000	0.0223
6. Textiles	321	0.0000	0.0022	0.0035	0.0001	0.0007	0.0000	0.0209
7. Clothing	322	0.0017	0.0006	0.0000	0.0002	0.0012	0.0002	0.1251
8. Leather Products	323	0.0000	0.0000	0.0040	0.0000	0.0000	0.0000	0.0309
9. Footwear	324	0.0000	0.0000	0.0000	0.0000	0.0015	0.0000	0.0000
10. Wood Products	331	0.0106	0.6240	0.0535	0.0018	0.0001	0.0000	0.0008
11. Furniture Fixtures	332	0.0024	0.0062	0.0001	0.0041	0.0007	0.0006	0.3813
12. Paper Products	341	0.0033	0.0052	0.0352	0.0031	0.0134	0.0050	0.0403
13. Printing and Publishing	342	0.0031	0.0170	0.0411	0.0016	0.0432	0.0120	0.3515
14. Fertilizer	35A	0.0000	0.0070	0.0007	0.0000	0.0000	0.0000	0.0042
15. Other Chemicals	35B	0.0011	0.0693	0.0023	0.0000	0.0006	0.0000	0.1003
16. Petroleum Products	35C	0.0192	0.0031	0.0031	0.0244	0.1993	0.0009	0.0033
17. Rubber Products	355	0.0005	0.0054	0.0024	0.0001	0.1657	0.0006	0.0005
18. Non-metallic Mineral Products	36A	0.0000	0.8822	0.0012	0.0000	0.0000	0.0000	0.0001
19. Glass Products	362	0.0088	0.3672	0.0000	0.0068	0.0009	0.0000	0.0173
20. Iron and Steel	371	0.0037	0.3240	0.0055	0.0048	0.0126	0.0000	0.0012
21. Non-ferrous Metal	372	0.0010	0.0000	0.0058	0.0000	0.0000	0.0000	0.0272
22. Metal Products	381	0.0057	0.0038	0.0259	0.0265	0.0091	0.0000	0.0184
23. Non-electrical Machinery	382	0.0110	0.0040	0.0013	0.0010	0.0063	0.0016	0.0018
24. Electrical Machinery	383	0.0275	0.1042	0.0015	0.0092	0.0174	0.0004	0.0061
25. Transport Equipment	384	0.0004	0.0029	0.0021	0.1113	0.0914	0.0071	0.0009
26. Miscellaneous Manufacturing	38A	0.0195	0.0060	0.0130	0.0005	0.0127	0.0001	0.1331
27. Mining and Quarrying	2	0.1255	0.1360	0.0012	0.0089	0.0014	0.0000	0.0173
28. Electricity, Gas and Water	4	0.2480	0.0453	0.0244	0.0154	0.0208	0.0071	0.0268
29. Construction	5	0.0074	0.0001	0.0042	0.0141	0.0064	0.0496	0.0084
30. Wholesale and Retail Trade	6	0.0129	0.0768	0.0142	0.0024	0.0162	0.0010	0.0287
31. Rail Transport	7A	0.0683	0.0797	0.0180	0.0080	0.0241	0.0026	0.0135
32. Other Transport, Storage and Communication	7B	0.0081	0.0383	0.1411	0.0029	0.0628	0.0005	0.0469
33. Finance, Insurance, and Real Estate	8	0.0035	0.0160	0.0419	0.0080	0.0269	0.0014	0.0545
34. Commercial, Social and Personal Services	9	0.0014	0.0152	0.0356	0.0025	0.0117	0.0003	0.0209

vd(i,j) : Intermediate demand for good i by industry j's share of total purchases of good i in India (unit : decimal fraction)

Table 20. Elasticity (Demand)

SN SECTOR	ISIC Code	eta (j) Michigan	Ours
1. Paddy	1A		
2. Wheat	1B		
3. Other Cereals	1C		
4. Rest of Agriculture	1D		
5. Food, Beverage and Tobacco	310	-1.1345	-1.0082
6. Textiles	321	-1.1478	-1.0148
7. Clothing	322	-5.0137	-2.9888
8. Leather Products	323	-1.6679	-1.3327
9. Footwear	324	-4.5184	-2.7294
10. Wood Products	331	-1.7421	-1.0080
11. Furniture Fixtures	332	-3.2495	-0.9809
12. Paper Products	341	-1.5873	-0.9804
13. Printing and Publishing	342	-3.0143	-1.0082
14. Fertilizer	35A	-2.6147	-1.1559
15. Other Chemicals	35B	-2.6168	-1.1560
16. Petroleum Products	35C	-2.0006	-1.0594
17. Rubber Products	355	-5.6902	-2.1820
18. Non-metallic Mineral Products	36A	-2.8077	-1.8999
19. Glass Products	362	-1.6467	-1.3160
20. Iron and Steel	371	-1.4636	-0.9707
21. Non-ferrous Metal	372	-1.4318	-0.8743
22. Metal Products	381	-3.6990	-1.4161
23. Non-electrical Machinery	382	-1.0225	-1.0039
24. Electrical Machinery	383	-2.3421	-1.1505
25. Transport Equipment	384	-3.6800	-1.2281
26. Miscellaneous Manufacturing	38A	-1.9223	-1.0234
27. Mining and Quarrying	2		-0.6574
28. Electricity, Gas and Water	4		-1.0000
29. Construction	5		
30. Wholesale and Retail Trade	6		
31. Rail Transport	7A		
32. Other Transport, Storage and Communication	7B		
33. Finance, Insurance, and Real Estate	8		
34. Commercial, Social and Personal Services	9		

eta(j) : Percieved elasticity of demand by a firm in sector j in India (unit : elasticity)

Table 21. Factor Shares of Expenditure

SN	SECTOR	ISIC Code	thetaL1(j)	thetaK1(j)	Total
1.	Paddy	1A			
2.	Wheat	1B			
3.	Other Cereals	1C			
4.	Rest of Agriculture	1D			
5.	Food, Beverage and Tobacco	310	0.3359	0.6641	1.0000
6.	Textiles	321	0.5250	0.4750	1.0000
7.	Clothing	322	0.3047	0.6953	1.0000
8.	Leather Products	323	0.3910	0.609	1.0000
9.	Footwear	324	0.5427	0.4573	1.0000
10.	Wood Products	331	0.4822	0.5178	1.0000
11.	Furniture Fixtures	332	0.8076	0.1924	1.0000
12.	Paper Products	341	0.3060	0.6940	1.0000
13.	Printing and Publishing	342	0.6094	0.3906	1.0000
14.	Fertilizer	35A	0.2681	0.7319	1.0000
15.	Other Chemicals	35B	0.2868	0.7132	1.0000
16.	Petroleum Products	35C	0.1055	0.8945	1.0000
17.	Rubber Products	355	0.3532	0.6468	1.0000
18.	Non-metallic Mineral Products	36A	0.3186	0.6814	1.0000
19.	Glass Products	362	0.4030	0.5970	1.0000
20.	Iron and Steel	371	0.0800	0.9200	1.0000
21.	Non-ferrous Metal	372	0.2875	0.7125	1.0000
22.	Metal Products	381	0.4056	0.5944	1.0000
23.	Non-electrical Machinery	382	0.4350	0.5650	1.0000
24.	Electrical Machinery	383	0.3660	0.634	1.0000
25.	Transport Equipment	384	0.5622	0.4378	1.0000
26.	Miscellaneous Manufacturing	38A	0.3251	0.6749	1.0000
27.	Mining and Quarrying	2	0.4100	0.59	1.0000
28.	Electricity, Gas and Water	4	0.4559	0.5441	1.0000
29.	Construction	5	0.7390	0.261	1.0000
30.	Wholesale and Retail Trade	6	0.4300	0.57	1.0000
31.	Rail Transport	7A	0.9329	0.0671	1.0000
32.	Other Transport, Storage and Communication	7B	0.4100	0.59	1.0000
33.	Finance, Insurance, and Real Estate	8	0.4100	0.59	1.0000
34.	Commercial, Social and Personal Services	9	0.9100	0.09	1.0000

theta L1(j) : Labor's share of expenditure on primary inputs in sector j (unit : decimal fraction)
theta K1(j) : Capital's share of expenditure on primary inputs in sector j (unit : decimal fraction)

(continued)

Table 21. *(Continued)*

SN SECTOR	ISIC Code	thetaF3(j)	thetaK3(j)	thetaL2(j)	thetaKF2(j)
1. Paddy	1A	0.7250	0.2750	0.4030	0.5970
2. Wheat	1B	0.6136	0.3864	0.3016	0.6984
3. Other Cereals	1C	0.6117	0.3883	0.3562	0.6438
4. Rest of Agriculture	1D	0.7209	0.2791	0.3768	0.6232
5. Food, Beverage and Tobacco	310				
6. Textiles	321				
7. Clothing	322				
8. Leather Products	323				
9. Footwear	324				
10. Wood Products	331				
11. Furniture Fixtures	332				
12. Paper Products	341				
13. Printing and Publishing	342				
14. Fertilizer	35A				
15. Other Chemicals	35B				
16. Petroleum Products	35C				
17. Rubber Products	355				
18. Non-metallic Mineral Products	36A				
19. Glass Products	362				
20. Iron and Steel	371				
21. Non-ferrous Metal	372				
22. Metal Products	381				
23. Non-electrical Machinery	382				
24. Electrical Machinery	383				
25. Transport Equipment	384				
26. Miscellaneous Manufacturing	38A				
27. Mining and Quarrying	2				
28. Electricity, Gas and Water	4				
29. Construction	5				
30. Wholesale and Retail Trade	6				
31. Rail Transport	7A				
32. Other Transport, Storage and Communication	7B				
33. Finance, Insurance, and Real Estate	8				
34. Commercial, Social and Personal Services	9				

theta F3(j): Land's share of expenditure on 2nd stage aggregate of primary inputs in sector j (unit: decimal fraction)
theta K3(j): Capital's share of expenditure on second stage of primary inputs in sector j (unit: decimal fraction)
theta L2(j): Labor's share of expenditure on 1st stage aggregate of primary inputs in sector j (unit: decimal fraction)
thetaKF2(j): Share of composite land / capital expenditure on 1st stage aggregate of primary input (unit: decimal fraction)

Table 22. Cost Shares

SN SECTOR	ISIC Code	thetaMC(j)	thetaFC(j)	thetaVK(j)
1. Paddy	1A	1.0000	0.0000	
2. Wheat	1B	1.0000	0.0000	
3. Other Cereals	1C	1.0000	0.0000	
4. Rest of Agriculture	1D	1.0000	0.0000	
5. Food, Beverage and Tobacco	310	0.8656	0.1344	0.7644
6. Textiles	321	0.7157	0.2843	1.1213
7. Clothing	322	0.8075	0.1925	0.3046
8. Leather Products	323	0.9484	0.0516	0.3696
9. Footwear	324	0.6336	0.3664	0.9496
10. Wood Products	331	0.8413	0.1587	0.6860
11. Furniture Fixtures	332	0.4324	0.5676	1.5119
12. Paper Products	341	0.6248	0.3753	2.2209
13. Printing and Publishing	342	0.9612	0.0388	0.1035
14. Fertilizer	35A	0.8216	0.1784	0.9864
15. Other Chemicals	35B	0.8216	0.1784	0.7837
16. Petroleum Products	35C	0.9944	0.0057	0.1111
17. Rubber Products	355	0.7708	0.2292	0.8654
18. Non-metallic Mineral Products	36A	0.7386	0.2614	0.9966
19. Glass Products	362	0.6331	0.3669	0.8268
20. Iron and Steel	371	0.7836	0.2164	0.8518
21. Non-ferrous Metal	372	0.8726	0.1274	0.7595
22. Metal Products	381	0.5036	0.4964	1.0593
23. Non-electrical Machinery	382	0.7377	0.2623	0.8790
24. Electrical Machinery	383	0.6446	0.3554	0.9219
25. Transport Equipment	384	0.6591	0.3409	0.9268
26. Miscellaneous Manufacturing	38A	0.8067	0.1933	0.5660
27. Mining and Quarrying	2	0.3545	0.6455	0.9744
28. Electricity, Gas and Water	4	0.6252	0.3748	0.9172
29. Construction	5	1.0000	0.0000	0.0000
30. Wholesale and Retail Trade	6	1.0000	0.0000	0.0000
31. Rail Transport	7A	1.0000	0.0000	0.0000
32. Other Transport, Storage and Communication	7B	1.0000	0.0000	0.0000
33. Finance, Insurance, and Real Estate	8	1.0000	0.0000	0.0000
34. Commercial, Social and Personal Services	9	1.0000	0.0000	0.0000

thetaMC(j): Variable input share of total cost in sector j (unit : decimal fraction)
thetaFC(j): Fixed input share of total cost in sector j (unit : decimal fraction)
thetaVK(j): Variable capital's share of total capital employed in sector j (unit : decimal fraction)

Name Index

Subject Index

STUDIES IN INTERNATIONAL TRADE POLICY

Studies in International Trade Policy includes works dealing with the theory, empirical analysis, political, economic, legal relations, and evaluations of international trade policies and institutions.

General Editor: Robert M. Stern

John H. Jackson and Edwin Vermulst, Editors. *Antidumping Law and Practice: A Comparative Study*

John Whalley, Editor. *Developing Countries and the Global Trading System.* Volumes 1 and 2

John Whalley, Coordinator. *The Uruguay Round and Beyond: The Final Report from the Ford Foundation Project on Developing Countries and the Global Trading System*

John S. Odell and Thomas D. Willett, Editors. *International Trade Policies: Gains from Exchange between Economics and Political Science*

Ulrich Kohli. *Technology, Duality, and Foreign Trade: The GNP Function Approach to Modeling Imports and Exports*

Stephen V. Marks and Keith E. Maskus, Editors. *The Economics and Politics of World Sugar Policies*

J. Michael Finger, Editor. *Antidumping: How It Works and Who Gets Hurt*

Horst Herberg and Ngo Van Long, Editors. *Trade, Welfare, and Economic Policies: Essays in Honor of Murray C. Kemp*

David Schwartzman. *The Japanese Television Cartel: A Study Based on* Matsushita v. Zenith

Alan V. Deardorff and Robert M. Stern, Editors. *Analytical Perspectives and Negotiating Issues in the Global Trading System*

Edwin Vermulst, Paul Waer, and Jacques Bourgeois, Editors. *Rules of Origin in International Trade: A Comparative Study*

Alan V. Deardorff and Robert M. Stern, Editors. *The Stolper-Samuelson Theorem: A Golden Jubilee*

Kent Albert Jones. *Export Restraint and the New Protectionism: The Political Economy of Discriminatory Trade Restrictions*

Alan V. Deardorff, James A. Levinsohn, and Robert M. Stern, Editors. *New Directions in Trade Theory*

Robert Baldwin, Tain-Jy Chen, and Douglas Nelson. *Political Economy of U.S.–Taiwan Trade*

Bernard M. Hoekman and Petros C. Mavroidis, Editors. *Law and Policy in Public Purchasing: The WTO Agreement on Government Procurement*

Danny M. Leipziger, Editor. *Lessons from East Asia*

Tamin Bayoumi. *Financial Integration and Real Activity*

Harry P. Bowen, Abraham Hollander, and Jean-Marie Viaene. *Applied International Trade Analysis*